WASHINGTON D.C.

CITY OF MANY DREAMS

Featuring the photography of Robert Van Der Hilst

First English edition published by Colour Library International Ltd.
© 1983 Illustrations and Text: Colour Library International Ltd.
 99 Park Avenue, New York, N.Y. 10016, U.S.A.
This edition is published by Crescent Books
Distributed by Crown Publishers, Inc.
h g f e d c b a
Colour separations by FER-CROM, Barcelona, Spain.
Display and text filmsetting by ACESETTERS LTD., Richmond, Surrey, England.
Printed and bound in Barcelona, Spain by Cayfosa and EUROBINDER
ISBN 0-517-405490
CRESCENT 1983

WASHINGTON D.C.

CITY OF MANY DREAMS

Text by MARVIN KARP

Designed by GARY HAZELL

Produced by
TED SMART and DAVID GIBBON

CRESCENT BOOKS

This is the tale of a city – a very special city called Washington, D.C.

Conceived and built as the embodiment of the hopes and aspirations of a freedom-loving people . . . and an idealistic dreamer . . . it truly deserves the sobriquet, "City of Dreams." Never before had a city been created specifically to be the capital of a country, but nothing else would do for the citizens of the brash young nation that had just won its independence from England. They had risked everything for the right to formulate a new system of self-government, and they were determined to erect a suitable capital for their fledgling nation on a new foundation, unencumbered by past influences and traditions.

Now, almost two centuries later, millions of tourists visit this handsome mecca of democracy every year and stand in awe before the edifices, the monuments and the statuary that commemorate the significant milestones in this nation's history. But only those who know the origin of the city will appreciate the temerity and foresightedness of the men who brought this legacy into being, and the dedication of those who helped perpetuate it. Washington is much more than a collection of stone and bronze memorials; it is the end result of the faith and foibles, the self-interest and sacrifices, the patriotism and politicking of those Americans who have had their moment in history while serving in those two aged bulwarks of freedom, the White House and the Capitol.

The idea to build a Federal City started in 1783, when the area on which this city now stands was covered by a large, densely-wooded forest, bordered by swampland and marshes. At that time, the Continental Congress, then sitting in Annapolis, Maryland, appointed a commission to select a site for a national capital of the newly-independent United States. Ever since its first meeting in 1774, the Congress had convened in a different city almost every session, and the legislators were beginning to feel more like itinerant peddlers than lawmakers. Unfortunately, the commission did nothing to alleviate that situation.

Then, at the Constitutional Convention in Philadelphia in 1787, the issue of a permanent home was included in that document under Article 1, Section VIII, Subsection 17, which states:

"Congress shall have the power to exercise exclusive legislation in all cases whatsoever, over such district (not exceeding ten miles square) as may, by cession of particular States, and the acceptance of Congress, become the seat of the Government of the United States, and to exercise like authority over all places purchased by the consent of the legislature of the State in which the same shall be, for the erection of forts, magazines, arsenals, dockyards and other needful buildings."

But committing their need to paper did not resolve the situation for the legislators. In fact, it had the opposite effect. Sectional feelings were so intense about where the capital should be located that the issue almost split the country in half. Representatives of the Southern states advocated a site on the Potomac River between Maryland and Virginia. Northerners, whose interests were more industrial than agrarian, argued that the Federal District should be located in or near a center of finance and commerce like Philadelphia or New York. Neither group could prevail until Alexander Hamilton and Thomas Jefferson worked out a compromise that included another important, but unresolved, issue of the day.

As Secretary of the Treasury and one of the principal voices of the Federalist Party, Hamilton was trying to persuade Congress to pass a bill that would authorize the Federal Government to assume the wartime debts of the states and to borrow enough money from other countries to pay the interest those debts had accrued. The debts, in the form of state-issued bonds, added up to the not-inconsiderable sum of $20,000,000. Anti-Federalist Southern planters and landowners, led by Secretary of State Thomas Jefferson, believed that the federal assumption of state debts was a plot to benefit those wealthy New Englanders who had speculated in war bonds.

Hamilton and Jefferson met for dinner one evening and concluded an agreement that gave each faction what it wanted most. The Federalists got enough Southern votes to pass the assumption bill; the anti-Federalists received Northern support to insure the location of the proposed Federal City on the Potomac.

In anticipation of the compromise, the Maryland legislature passed "An act to cede to Congress a District of ten miles square in this State, for the Seat of Government of the United States." And Virginia followed shortly thereafter with "An act for the cession of ten miles square, or any lesser quantity of territory within this State to the United States in Congress assembled, for the permanent seat of the General Government."

The final step was taken on July 16, 1790, when George

Washington, who had been sworn in the previous year as the first President of the United States, signed the Residence Act, which authorized the purchase of land somewhere along the Potomac River for the Federal District. The act was amended the following year to give Washington the final word in choosing the actual site. The act also stipulated that the President could appoint a committee of three to oversee the planning and construction of the city, which was to be named after Mr. Washington. And it stated that "suitable buildings for the accommodation of Congress, and of the President, and for the public offices of the government" be ready for occupancy prior to the first Monday in December, 1800. During the interim years, the government would sit in Philadelphia.

Washington had the option of creating the Federal District anywhere along a 100-mile stretch of the Potomac River. He decided on the ten-mile-square area below the Potomac's falls, where the Eastern Branch (now known as the Anacostia River) converged with the Potomac. He chose this location because the river was navigable for commercial traffic at that time, and he wanted the new city to be a deep water port. Coincidentally, the city would be an easy day's ride from Washington's home, Mount Vernon.

The proposed site, three-fifths of which lay in Maryland and the remainder in Virginia, included George Town, which was a port in Maryland and the home of the recently-founded Jesuit school, Georgetown University, plus the settlements of Carrollsburg and Hamburg, and the port city of Alexandria in Virginia.

Once he had selected the site, Washington wasted no time in setting the project in motion. He named as his commissioners three gentlemen who knew the territory and the local landowners. They were Daniel Carroll and Thomas Johnson of Maryland, and Dr. David Stuart of Virginia. He assigned the task of surveying the area and fixing the boundaries of the city to Andrew Ellicott, a highly-regarded public surveyor, and Benjamin Banneker, a black freedman who was a publisher, mathematician and astronomer. And last, but not least, the President asked Major Pierre Charles L'Enfant, whom Washington persisted in calling "Langfang," to draw up a master plan for the city proper. This latter choice proved to be both inspired ... and unfortunate, as Washington soon found out.

Pierre Charles L'Enfant, engineer, architect and soldier, was born in France, and, like his countryman, the Marquis de Lafayette, crossed the Atlantic Ocean to help the American colonies win their independence. L'Enfant volunteered as a private in the army, attained the rank of captain and was wounded leading a charge at Charleston. He was captured, exchanged for a Hessian officer and returned to France where King Louis XVI decorated and promoted him. L'Enfant then declined a commission in the French army to return to

his adopted country. He came to Washington's attention when he designed the insignia of the Society of Cincinnati, and later remodeled the city hall in New York City to serve as a temporary seat of the Federal government. When he learned of the government's intention to build its national capital in the wilderness, L'Enfant wrote to Washington, asking for the privilege of developing the plans for the city "which is to become the Capital of this vast Empire." In March, 1791, L'Enfant was informed by Thomas Jefferson that the job was his. Immediately thereafter, L'Enfant could be seen criss-crossing the site on foot and horseback, studying the topography, and keeping his own counsel.

At the same time, Washington and his commissioners convinced the landowners of the property within the Federal District to sell to the government the land it needed for building purposes at the bargain price of $67 an acre, and to donate without charge the land designated for roads and streets. In return, the landowners would retain the commercial rights to the remaining property in the area whose value would be greatly enhanced by their location in what was expected to be a boom town.

Meanwhile, with an eye to the future and a total disregard for the practicalities of the moment, L'Enfant went about drawing up plans "on such a scale as to leave room for that aggrandizement and embellishment which the increase of wealth of the nation will permit it to pursue to any period however remote." He lived by the philosophy, "Make no little plans." Toward that end, and with Washington's approval, he selected the highest point in the area, a flat-topped promontory over 80 feet in height named Jenkins' Hill, as the site for the Capitol, which he called the "Congress House." Next, he located the "President's Palace" a mile away on the flat, low ground near a small body of water known as Tiber Creek, where it would have a fine view of the Potomac. The two buildings were to be linked by Pennsylvania Avenue, a triumphal boulevard measuring 160 feet across. Just south of the residence for the President, L'Enfant planned a capacious mall that would extend back to the Capitol. Then, he drew a system of broad avenues and thoroughfares that radiated from the Capitol like spokes of a wheel and cut through a conventional rectangular grid of streets. His reasons for creating this pattern were threefold: first, the wide avenues would provide direct, rapid access to the Capitol; next, their openness would offer an opportunity to create charming plazas and erect statuary along their routes, thereby bringing a feeling of elegance and grace to the city; and lastly, taking a lesson from the street riots in Paris during the French Revolution, the Capitol could be more easily defended from its position as the elevated hub of the spokes.

When L'Enfant's overall plans were revealed, the landowners and the commissioners were stunned by his extravagance. Of the more than 6,600 acres within the agreed-upon boundaries of the Federal City, fewer than 600 acres were designated as sites to be purchased for government buildings. Almost 3,700 acres were to be utilized, without compensation to the owners, for the construction of L'Enfant's majestic avenues and the enormous mall. This left little more than 1,900 acres for the owners to cut up and sell as commercial plots. The only point of mutual agreement between L'Enfant and the commissioners was the designation of the avenues and streets. The diagonal avenues were to be named after the 13 original states. Washington would be divided into four sections, with the streets based on a north-south, east-west grid and the Capitol at the center. North-south streets were to be numbered; east-west streets were to be given letters of the alphabet.

The outraged landowners made their complaints known to the President through his commissioners, but Washington chose to ignore them. Unable to effect an accommodation with Washington or L'Enfant, the property owners decided to auction off the 1,900 acres they still controlled. But, once again, the stubborn Frenchman frustrated and angered them. Fearful that speculators would buy up the lots and erect cheap, unsightly commercial structures alongside or near his prized avenues and spoil the effect of his grand design, L'Enfant withheld his blueprint of the city from the sellers.

Then, shortly thereafter, L'Enfant's intransigence finally brought on predictably unpleasant consequences. He had begun clearing paths through the forest for Pennsylvania Avenue and other major arteries when his work crew found a manor house under construction that extended into one avenue's right-of-way. Though he knew that the new house was the property of Daniel Carroll of Duddington, a close relative of Commissioner Carroll, the largest landowner in the area, L'Enfant ordered the intruding structure razed. He did so despite instructions from the commissioners to desist, and an injunction from the Chancellor of Maryland.

That incident plus L'Enfant's continued reluctance to provide plans of the city for use at a public auction, led his patron and protector, George Washington, to say: "I did not expect to meet with such perverseness in Major L'Enfant, as his late conduct exhibited." By now, L'Enfant had alienated so many powerful people, including Thomas Jefferson, that Washington regretfully agreed to rescind his commission. And so, on March 14, 1792, a year after he had begun his monumental task, Pierre Charles L'Enfant received a communication from the commissioners that stated: "We have been notified that we are no longer to consider you as engaged in the business of the Federal City."

L'Enfant was crushed by his dismissal and refused the commissioners' offer of 500 guineas (approximately $2,500) plus a city lot as compensation for his efforts. He later also refused an appointment as Professor of Engineering at West Point. (The record does show, however, that by a Congressional act of May 1, 1810, he did receive almost $1,400 for his services in laying out the city of Washington.) But from the day he was relieved of his duties, L'Enfant had just one purpose in life – to be reinstated on the project. Towards the end, his tall, gaunt figure in a long blue military coat and high beaver hat could be seen trudging around the construction sites, and haunting the Rotunda of the Capitol seeking redress that was not to be. Finally, on June 14, 1825, this proud, visionary Frenchman died, never knowing that, except for some minimal changes, the essence of his dream would become the heart of Washington, D.C.

At the time L'Enfant was dismissed, the responsibility for completing the plans of the city fell to the surveyor, Andrew Ellicott. But, he too incurred the displeasure of the commissioners who complained to Washington about Ellicott's absenteeism. On January 28, 1794, the commissioners informed the President that "we discharged him (Ellicott) at our last meeting." For the most part, however, the plans were complete enough for the city to start taking shape.

Concurrent with overseeing the preparation of plans for the city, the commissioners had been pushing ahead with their quest for suitable building plans. Once Jenkins' Hill, which L'Enfant had described as "a pedestal waiting for a monument," had been approved as the site for the Capitol, the President urged them to expedite the solicitation of architectural designs for the building. They responded by placing an advertisement in the principal newspapers of the country announcing "a premium of a lot in this city to be designated by impartial judges, and five hundred dollars, or a medal of that value at the option of the party, will be given by the Commissioners of the Federal Buildings to the person who before the 15th of July, 1792, shall produce to them the most approved plan for a Capitol to be erected in this city; and two hundred and fifty dollars, or a medal, to the plan deemed next in merit to the one they shall adopt."

The public competition elicited about 16 submissions from architects, draftsmen and assorted amateurs, and from among them, the plan of Étienne Hallet, a French architect, who had moved to Philadelphia before the Revolution, appeared to be the winner. Hallet was invited to inspect the proposed site and encouraged to make last-minute alterations in his plan in keeping with suggestions from the President and other interested parties. But then, when it seemed that Hallet's design was about to be accepted, and long after the expiration date for the competition, a Dr. William Thornton submitted a plan that, in the words of Thomas Jefferson, "Captivated the eyes and judgment of all." It also met with the approbation of George Washington, who was enthusiastic about its "grandeur, simplicity and convenience," and recommended its acceptance by the commissioners. It was essentially a simple design showing two wings on either side of a central portion, fronted by columns and topped by a low dome.

In April, 1793, the commissioners informed Thornton that the

President had approved his plans, making him the official winner of the design competition. At the same time, to ease Hallet's disappointment, the commissioners offered to compensate him for his time and effort. In addition, they gave Hallet the job of overseeing the construction of the Capitol, because they knew Thornton was not a professional architect. So, it came about that on September 18, 1793, a date marking the 18th year of American independence, a significant event took place that few Americans remember. Amid the pomp and pageantry of marching bands and flying colors, George Washington, using a silver trowel, laid the cornerstone of the proposed north, or Senate, wing of the Capitol. An integral part of the ceremony was a Masonic procession led by the President wearing a Masonic apron that had been sewn by Madame de Lafayette. It was duly reported in the local newspaper that, following the appropriate speeches and ceremonial volleys by the Alexandria volunteer artillery, the participants feasted on a 500-pound barbecued ox.

Just as the laying of the cornerstone has been obscured by time, so too has the man who designed the Capitol, although he was not unknown in his own day. Born on Tortola, the largest island in the group now called the British Virgin Islands, William Thornton was educated in England, where he earned a medical degree before emigrating to New York in 1787. There is no record of his ever having practised medicine in America, but the record does show him to be a man of many interests and talents. For example, learning in 1789 that the Library Company of Philadelphia was offering an award for the best design for its proposed new building, Dr. Thornton "got some books and worked a few days, then gave a plan in the ancient Ionic order, which carried the day." At the same time, he was working with inventor John Fitch to design the first commercial steamboat.

After winning the competition for the Capitol, Dr. Thornton moved to the city of Washington, where he became a successful architectural designer of private homes, among them the Octagon House which not only had a role in history but is still standing. In 1802, the multi-talented doctor began another career when President Jefferson appointed him to the position of clerk in charge of patents. He later became the first Superintendent of Patents, a position he held until his death in 1828. He is considered the "Father of the Patent Office."

When the serious work of constructing the north wing got underway, Étienne Hallet began to make changes in Dr. Thornton's original plans without proper authority or approval. The relationship between the two men quickly deteriorated and reached the point where the commissioners were forced to admonish Hallet in a letter, stating: "... in general, nothing has ever gone from us by which we intended or we believe you could infer that you ... or anybody else were to introduce into that building any departures from Dr. Thornton's plan without the President's or Commissioners' approbation..." Shortly afterwards, Hallet was relieved of his duties. He was replaced in 1795 by a student at London's Royal Academy named George Hadfield, who was given a two-year work contract. Just prior to Hadfield's appointment, Dr. Thornton was named a Commissioner of Federal Buildings, a position that gave him greater authority to see that his plans were carried out.

Once again, the man who had only contracted to supervise the construction of the building felt compelled to impose some of his own ideas on the architect's plans. When he was rebuffed, Hadfield threatened to resign even though he still had several months to go under the terms of his contract. He was a very surprised young man when the authorities made no effort to dissuade him and even offered to buy his passage back to England immediately. Hadfield quickly reconsidered and continued on the job until his contract expired. He remained in Washington but never came into public prominence again.

The next construction supervisor was James Hoban, a native of Ireland who had settled in Charleston, South Carolina, before the Revolution. A trained architect, Hoban had entered a competition to design the President's House, which was conducted at the same time the contest for the Capitol was held. He took the first prize of $500 and a city lot. Hoban's clean, simple design of a rectangular, two-story building with symmetrical rows of tall windows won over many other entries, including one from Thomas Jefferson who had submitted it anonymously, using only the initials "A.Z." Construction of the President's House was begun immediately, so, from the time he replaced Hadfield, until 1802, Hoban was responsible for the progress made on both buildings.

Despite personnel changes, previously bungled construction that Hoban had to have redone, and a shortage of building funds that the state of Maryland covered by running a lottery, progress was made on the two most important structures in the city. Then, late in the summer of 1800, Congress and the President were notified that it was time to start packing and to prepare to vacate Philadelphia for their new homes. The north wing of the Capitol and the President's House were not quite finished, but they could be occupied in November. This news was not greeted with much enthusiasm by most members of the government, and the grumbling could be heard even in the temporary quarters of the Presidential family. After enjoying the comforts of life in Philadelphia, the legislators were reluctant to exchange those amenities for the discomforts they could anticipate in the primitive city in the wilderness. This was particularly true of John Adams, who followed George Washington as the second President after Washington's second term ended in 1796. Adams knew that he had not been re-elected in 1800, which meant he would be out of office just a few months after moving his family to the new capital. But, like it or not, in compliance with the Constitutional timetable, all the records, archives and furniture belonging to the infant republic were loaded aboard a small river sloop, and the seat of government sailed up the Potomac to Washington, D.C.

What was the city like in the fall of 1800? According to one report, there were 372 houses scattered on lots throughout the area, 109 constructed of brick and 263 of wood. Total population: about 3,000. Lodgings for the incoming legislators near the Capitol were minimal, forcing many of them to reside in Georgetown, which, though only three miles away, was difficult to reach because of the bad roads. Pennsylvania Avenue, for example, was described as "a deep morass covered with alder bushes." Governor Morris of New York wrote: "We want nothing here but houses, cellars, kitchens, well-informed men, amiable women and other trifles of this kind to make our city perfect."

It was John Adams, still dubious about the whole Washington venture, who composed a prayer on moving into the official mansion. This prayer, which President Franklin Delano Roosevelt ordered carved into the mantel in the State Dining Room more than 130 years later, reads: "I pray Heaven to bestow the best of Blessings on this House and all that shall hereafter inhabit it. May none but honest and wise Men ever rule under this roof."

On November 22, 1800, President Adams, formally attired, rode in a coach with outriders to Capitol Hill, as Jenkins' Hill was now known. At noon, he entered the Senate Chamber in the north wing of the Capitol and addressed a joint session of Congress. His welcoming remarks included the "hope that any inconvenience will cease with the present session," and he congratulated Congress "on the prospect of a residence not to be changed." There were 32 Senators and 105 Representatives in attendance.

In addition to the Congress, the personnel and activities of the Supreme Court, the Circuit Court and the Library of Congress were also crowded into the one building. It was not until seven years later that the south wing of the Capitol was completed, and the House of Representatives was able to move into its own permanent quarters.

Not only did the Adams Congress have the honor of being the first to sit in the national capital, it set another precedent soon after it convened by determining the next President of the United States. According to the Constitution, the electors in the electoral college were authorized to vote for a candidate by name but not by office, so the candidate receiving the most electoral votes automatically became President, with next highest vote-getter becoming Vice President. But a complication arose in the recently-concluded national election. Thomas Jefferson and Aaron Burr both received 73 electoral votes even though it was acknowledged that Jefferson was the Presidential candidate, with Burr running for the second spot. John Adams was third with 65 votes, and therefore out of contention. According to the Constitution, the job of determining which man should be President fell to the House of Representatives.

On February 17, 1801, after six days of closed-door meetings and 36 ballots, the deadlock was finally broken with 10 states going for Jefferson, four for Burr, and Delaware and South Carolina casting blank ballots. As a result of this confused situation, the 12th Amendment was enacted and ratified in 1804, calling for the electors to vote separately for President and Vice President. The House would be called on to determine the winner only if none of the top three candidates received a majority of the electoral votes. Such a situation occurred during the election of 1824 when neither John Quincy Adams, Henry Clay nor Andrew Jackson received an electoral majority. The election was decided in the House when Clay threw his support to Adams. Thus, the son of John and Abigail Adams became the sixth President.

Though sorely handicapped by the lack of comfortable surroundings and convivial environment, Abigail Adams felt it was her duty, as the First Lady, to establish social standards in Washington that were at least on the level of Philadelphia. She was determined that the nation's capital shed its backwoods image for one more worthy of its importance. With the aid and advice of the Widow Washington (her husband had died the previous year), Mrs. Adams, in proper New England and Federalist fashion, set up a dignified social salon in the Oval Room. There, she entertained each week. She also held the first full-scale formal reception in the President's House on New Year's Day of 1801. The President headed the receiving line wearing a black velvet suit with silk stockings, silver knee and shoe buckles, white waistcoat, powdered hair and gloves. Rather than shake hands with his guests, he bowed to them, following a tradition set by his predecessor, George Washington.

So, despite the dampness and discomfort of winter in the Potomac basin, Abigail Adams left her imprint on Washington society. And when the election of Thomas Jefferson was confirmed by the House, she quietly packed her belongings and retired to Massachusetts, leaving behind a courtly social system that future First Ladies might alter to suit their own personalities and life style, but never destroy.

John Adams worked until the stroke of twelve on March 3, 1801, the night preceding Jefferson's inauguration, signing papers that appointed Federalists to key judicial vacancies, a move that caused them to be derided as the "Midnight Judges." Adams then slipped out of the capital without attending the inauguration because of the enmity that had developed between himself and Jefferson based on their political differences. One supposition has been that he chose not to attend; another, that he was not invited.

Within a year after taking office, Jefferson named architect Benjamin Henry Latrobe to replace James Hoban in completing construction of the Capitol. He also worked with Latrobe to incorporate some of his ideas into the design for the mansion, ideas which he had nurtured ever since losing the competition to Hoban a decade earlier. Latrobe, a professional architect born in England and educated at the University of Leipzig, was well qualified for the job, having attained the position of Surveyor of Public Offices in London before arriving in America in 1796. He came to Jefferson's attention through his work on the penitentiary at Richmond and the Bank of Philadelphia. At the time of his appointment, Latrobe was involved in a riverfront project on the Potomac.

As a result of Jefferson's influence, Latrobe expanded the original plans for the mansion to include terraces extending from the east and west sides of the building, and porticoes facing north and south. These additions were not completed, however, until long after Jefferson was no longer President. Latrobe did complete the south wing of the Capitol, according to Thornton's plans, in time for the House of Representatives to meet there in October, 1807. He then built a wooden passageway to connect it to the north wing.

In keeping with his feelings about equality and democratic conventions, Jefferson made some interesting changes in Washington protocol. He abbreviated the social agenda at the Executive Mansion by reducing the formal entertaining and frequent drawing-room gatherings to just two mass celebrations a year, on the Fourth of July and New Year's Day. To the shock and chagrin of Washington's high society, Jefferson threw open the doors of the mansion at those times and invited the ordinary citizens to mingle with diplomats and government officials. He also did away with the custom of bowing when receiving people, preferring instead to shake hands.

He was uncomfortable with the Federalists' ostentation and opted for small dinners with selected friends at which he would serve rare wines and beautifully prepared meals based on his favorite French or Italian recipes. Being a widower, he would frequently ask Mrs. James (Dolley) Madison to act as his hostess. He insisted on a round or oval table to eliminate the protocol of seating according to rank. Jefferson also felt that dining would be more stimulating if all the guests could see and converse with each other.

In addition to his epicurean tastes, Jefferson had an excellent eye for design and color. One of his personal projects was to furnish as much of the mansion as he could before his tenancy expired. He managed to finish 23 rooms down to the last detail before his second term ended, and he had to make way for Dolley and James Madison in 1809.

Once she became the official hostess in her own right, Dolley Madison dominated the social life in the Presidential mansion, and Washington society in general, as no First Lady had done before her, and very few would after her. Having acted as Jefferson's hostess for the previous eight years, while her husband served as Secretary of State, Dolley understood the unique opportunity her position presented and decided to enjoy it to the fullest. In contrast to James Madison, a small (5'4"), somewhat reticent man who was more inclined to scholarship than sociability, Dolley was several inches taller, a handsome, statuesque, ebullient lady. She had a gift for putting people at ease and a flair for entertaining that soon made her Wednesday evening drawing-room gatherings the most notable events of the week. No matter how large the affair – they often attracted several hundred people – Dolley made everyone feel at home by her warmth, tact and an almost infallible ability to greet every guest by name regardless of how long ago they may have met.

Though Dolley was always self-effacing about her knowledge of events on Capitol Hill, she, nevertheless, had a firm finger on the political pulse of Washington. And, on more than one occasion, she was able to defuse a potentially volatile situation for the President by exerting her influence over the wives of Madison's political opponents. There was one situation, however, that had been building, like steam in a pressure cooker, and neither she nor the President could do anything to avert the explosion.

Great Britain and France were at war when Madison came into office, and each country tried to prevent neutral American ships from carrying on commerce with its enemy. When the merchantmen still conducted their business as usual, both warring countries began to stop U.S. ships on the high seas, seize their cargoes, and, in the case of Great Britain, impress American seamen into the Royal navy. It was this latter violation that roused American antipathy towards the English to a fighting fever. All U.S. attempts at negotiation and compromise failed, and on June 18, 1812, the "War Hawks," led by Henry Clay, mustered enough votes for Congress to issue a declaration of war against Great Britain.

The conflict, designated in the history books as the War of 1812, was not overwhelmingly popular in the United States, particularly in the Northeast, where it was dubbed "Mr. Madison's War" by his opponents. With his popularity at a very low ebb, Madison barely survived his bid for re-election that year. The final tally showed him with 90 electoral votes versus 89 for DeWitt Clinton, who ran as peace candidate. Many political savants, then and now, credit that narrow victory to Dolley and her influence over Henry Clay, who threw his support to Madison. As one analyst wrote later: "She saved the administration of her husband . . . but for her, DeWitt Clinton would have been chosen President in 1812."

She may have had enough influence to save her husband's political career, but Dolley could not save her next greatest love, the nation's capital. In August, 1814, a British fleet, commanded by Admiral Sir George Cockburn, appeared in Chesapeake Bay and landed a 4,500-man raiding party on the shores of the Patuxent River, about 35 miles southeast of Washington. The raiders, comprised of Redcoats under the command of General Robert Ross, and Royal Marines, routed a contingent of ill-trained and poorly-equipped militia at Bladensburg. Meeting almost no further resistance, the British continued on the road to Washington. When news of the British advance reached the capital, Congress fled in a panic. The President had already vacated the city to join his military staff in the field, leaving Dolley at home. She waited for him to return, but finally, reluctantly, as she wrote in a letter to her sister, she realized that she had to flee.

"Mr. Madison comes not. May God protect us! Two messengers covered with dust to bid me fly, but here I mean to wait for him . . . At this late hour a wagon has been procured and I have had it filled with plates and the most valuable portable articles belonging to the house. Whether it will reach its destination – the Bank of Maryland – or fall into the hands of British soldiery, events must determine. Our kind friend, Mr. Carroll, has come to hasten my departure, and is in a very bad humour with me because I insist in waiting until the large picture of General Washington is secured, and it requires to be unscrewed from the wall. This process was found too tedious for these perilous moments. I have ordered the frame to be broken and the canvas taken out. It is done; and the precious portrait placed in the hands of two gentlemen of New York for safekeeping.

"And now, my dear sister, I must leave this house, or the retreating army will make me a prisoner in it by filling up the road I am directed to take."

Shortly after Dolley made her escape, the British entered Washington virtually unopposed and proceeded to torch the city. The date: August 24. For the next two days, the British looted, burned and generally vandalized the capital, with special attention being paid to government buildings, and then moved on to Alexandria. The invaders were finally stopped at Fort McHenry, en route to Baltimore, an event that was immortalized by a young Washington attorney named Francis Scott Key. Detained aboard a British warship, he witnessed the naval bombardment of the fort, and when he saw the American flag still flying at dawn, he was inspired to write the verses that became the words of the American national anthem.

Three days after the British evacuated Washington, the Madisons, now reunited, and members of Congress returned to the city to assess the devastation and resume the functions of government. They found the Presidential mansion reduced to a shell of cracked and blackened walls. The Capitol, including both wings and the Library of Congress, was in ruins. In fact, every government building and

installation, except one, had sustained severe damage. The one exception was the building housing the Patent Office, which Dr. Thornton, who was then Superintendent of Patents, has been credited with saving. According to reports of the incident, when Dr. Thornton saw that the building was about to be burned, he confronted the British officer in charge. "Are you Englishmen, or Goths and Vandals?" he asked. "This is the Patent Office, the depository of the inventive genius of America, in which the whole civilized world is concerned. Would you destroy it?" The officer reconsidered, and the building was spared.

One other small consolation in a very grim and disheartening situation was literally a gift from the heavens. Soon after the torching got underway, a violent rainstorm of almost hurricane-strength blew in and prevented the fires from spreading and possibly burning out the entire city. When news of the devastation reached Europe, Britain was universally condemned for its barbaric and brutal actions. Even many Englishmen openly repudiated the acts of vandalism committed by their countrymen, and a leading newspaper stated: "Willingly would we throw a veil of oblivion over our transactions at Washington. The Cossacks spared Paris, but we spared not the Capital of America."

With its quarters in shambles, the First Family took up temporary residence in Octagon House (18th Street and New York Avenue), a beautiful town house designed and built by Dr. Thornton for John Tayloe, a wealthy planter and horse breeder. Congress convened in the Patent Office building that was already crowded with the City and General Post Office and what was left of the Congressional Library. Soon after, Congress moved to other temporary quarters in a large brick building, now the site of the Supreme Court Building, that came to be known as the "Brick Capitol." The inconveniences caused by this dislocation rekindled the hopes of those die-hard advocates who still wanted to establish the nation's capital elsewhere, preferably in the Northeast. But those hopes were short-lived when a resolution to move the capital was defeated in the House.

On the war front, Great Britain was feeling the strain financially and militarily of what had become an almost futile pursuit. So, it was with mutual relief that American and British negotiators met at Ghent, Belgium, and on December 24, 1814, signed a treaty ending the War of 1812. It was ratified by the U.S. Senate the next February. Before word of the treaty reached America, however, a British invasion force tried to capture New Orleans. The attackers were decisively defeated by the American defenders under General Andrew Jackson, in a battle that became the biggest American victory of the war. It made a national hero of Jackson and was a tremendous asset in his quest for the Presidency some years later.

On February 18, 1815, President Madison signed the Treaty of

Ghent in his office at the Octagon House. Now, with the war finally concluded, one of the President's first imperatives was to order the renovation of the Capitol and the Presidential mansion. To accomplish these tasks as quickly as possible, Benjamin Latrobe was commissioned to repair the Capitol, which he described as "a most magnificent ruin." At the same time, James Hoban undertook the restoration of the mansion according to his original plans. Meanwhile, Dolley Madison, her enthusiasm undiminished and her spirit undaunted by the lack of adequate facilities, resumed her reign as the undisputed leader of Washington society even as the President's second term was winding down.

Despite Latrobe's best efforts, the original Capitol was not ready for the inauguration of James Monroe. And because the Brick Capitol, the temporary home of Congress, did not have sufficient seating capacity, a new precedent was set. On March 4, 1817, President-elect Monroe was sworn in as the fifth President in the first inaugural held outdoors. The ceremony took place, before a crowd of approximately 7,000 people, on a platform erected on the east portico of the building.

Later, on Capitol Hill, a disagreement developed between Latrobe and Samuel Lane, the Commissioner of Public Buildings, over the amount of time the architect was devoting to his private affairs. Their differences were settled when Latrobe resigned in November, 1817, after restoring most of the Capitol's two wings. Latrobe's successor was Charles Bulfinch, a Bostonian and the first American-born architect to be in charge of the Capitol's construction.

Bulfinch completed the restoration of the two wings in time for Congress to convene in them in 1819. Then, following Dr. Thornton's original design, which had been somewhat altered by Latrobe and further amended by himself, Bulfinch supervised the construction of the central portion of the Capitol. This section, joining the two wings and featuring a domed Rotunda, was mostly completed by 1824. To mark the occasion, a grand reception honoring Lafayette was given on the premises. And as a further indication of the esteem in which Americans held him, Lafayette was accorded the privilege of being the first foreign dignitary to address a joint meeting of Congress.

The Office of Capitol Architect was officially abolished in 1828, but Bulfinch continued to supervise the work for another year until he was satisfied that the dome was properly sheathed in copper and the original Capitol was substantially restored and finished according to Dr. Thornton's 37-year-old plans.

As for the Presidential mansion, it was not ready for occupancy by Elizabeth and James Monroe until the latter part of 1817, and even then it still smelled of fresh white paint that covered the fire-scarred outer walls. Some historians attribute the cognomen, "White House," to that cosmetic application; others claim the name pre-dated the renovation. Regardless of the actual origin, it does appear that from that time on, the official residence of the First Family was referred to more and more as the White House. There has never been an Executive Order establishing the name, but President Teddy Roosevelt gave it semi-official status many years later by having it engraved on his stationery, a custom that has been followed ever since.

Though most of the mansion's furnishings had been destroyed by the fire, the Monroes were determined to have enough rooms ready in time for the New Year's reception in 1818. In order to meet that deadline, however, the President sold the government his own best furniture, household linens, dishes and silver, most of which had been painstakingly and lovingly collected during his tours as a diplomatic representative of the United States in London and Paris. These furnishings were later augmented by many others ordered from France. Many of these items were used in the White House for years afterwards, but the President did buy back some of the pieces at the end of his second term.

Along with filling the White House with furnishings from abroad, President Monroe abolished the informality encouraged by his Virginia predecessors for the more stately protocol favored in European royal courts. John Quincy Adams, then Secretary of State, noted in his diary that "the President observed the usual forms practised by European sovereigns" when receiving foreign ministers carrying formal messages from other heads of state.

"He receives them standing, dressed in a half-military uniform or a full suit of black. The Ministers are in full Court dress. He stands in the center of the drawing room, and I (Adams) accompany them, keeping the right hand. On receiving the letter, the President hands it, unopened, to me. The English Prince Regent had the same practice with Lord Castlereagh."

Mrs. Monroe also had the ability to project a regal and commanding presence. In fact, it was because of that ability that she was credited with saving Madame de Lafayette from the guillotine during the French Revolution some years earlier. James Monroe was Minister Plenipotentiary to France during that turbulent period. When Mrs. Monroe learned of Madame de Lafayette's imprisonment, she commandeered the official carriage of the United States Legation, and had herself driven to La Force prison where she demanded her friend be released. She was.

The re-opening of the White House was a gala event for the American people and Washington society. The National Intelligencer reported: "It was gratifying once more to salute the President of the United States with the compliments of the season in his appropriate residence, and the continuance of this Republican custom has given, as far as we have heard, very general satisfaction." Unfortunately, that "general satisfaction" did not last long because the rigid protocol of the White House led to controversy over the reluctance of the First Family to receive and return courtesy calls from elected officials, cabinet members and their wives. The Monroes also incurred the displeasure of Washington society because of the special attention accorded foreign diplomats at White House dinners. These issues became such points of contention that the capital's social leaders boycotted the drawing rooms of both Mrs. Monroe and Mrs. Adams. Happily, the situation was resolved before too long, and Mrs. Monroe's weekly salons were once again crowded to overflowing. The same was true of Mrs. Adams' parties.

While Washington society indulged in its intrigues and squabbles, the rest of the country was enjoying a period of expansion and growth, a time affectionately called an "era of good feeling." The President's popularity was so high that when he ran for re-election in 1820, he received all of the 232 electoral votes but one. The lone dissenter, Senator William Plumer of New Hampshire, cast his vote for John Quincy Adams. Some say he did this in protest against a unanimous election, asserting that only George Washington should ever have that unique honor. Others say he was protesting against the continuation of the Virginia dynasty of Presidents.

Monroe's second term officially started one day late because March 4, 1821, fell on a Sunday, so the inauguration was postponed until the following day. It was held in the Chamber of the House of Representatives rather than outdoors due to inclement weather, and for the first time the Marine Band was included in the program, an innovation that was adopted at all later inaugurations.

Soon after Monroe started his second term, the social schedule at the White House was cut back because Mrs. Monroe's health began to fail. Political activity became livelier, however, when five powerful men declared their intention of running for the Presidency in 1824. The men were: Secretary of State Adams, John C. Calhoun, Secretary of War, William Harris Crawford, Secretary of the Treasury, Speaker of the House Henry Clay, and General Andrew Jackson, then a Senator from Tennessee. Monroe wisely remained aloof, refusing to endorse any candidate in what became a bitterly-fought campaign. The President even went so far as to decline an invitation to a fancy dress ball that the Adams gave for Jackson on the anniversary of his victory at New Orleans. The party, with more than 1,000 guests in attendance, was one of the outstanding successes of the 1824 Washington social season, but it failed as a peace offering to Jackson.

Jackson won a plurality of the popular vote, and the electoral vote, but did not garner the mandatory majority. Of the 261 electoral votes representing 24 states, Jackson polled 99,

Adams 84, Crawford 41 and Clay 37. This threw the election into the House of Representatives, where Clay, with the fewest electoral votes was automatically eliminated. And because he disliked Jackson almost as much as Adams did, Clay gave his support to Adams. On February 5, 1825, John Quincy Adams was elected President with a majority of 13 states. He then urged his friends in the House to elect Jackson to the Vice Presidency as a way of keeping him under control politically since "the Vice Presidency was a station in which the General could hang no one, and need quarrel with no one." The office went to John C. Calhoun instead.

The Monroe years in Washington ended in a blaze of social activity occasioned by the visit of their old friend, General Lafayette. The White House, to which James Hoban had recently added the semicircular south portico, once again became the setting for dinners and balls all through the month of December, ending with a New Year's day reception on January 1, 1825. The climax of the celebration for Lafayette, however, occurred that night at Williamson's Hotel. It was attended by several hundred guests, including many members of both Houses, other government officials and President Monroe, who broke his own long-standing rule about appearing at such functions. The banquet was a most convivial affair, with 16 toasts being drunk to the guest of honor.

Two months later, on March 4, two carriages, one carrying the President-elect and the other President Monroe, were accompanied to Capitol Hill by a military escort. At noon, Chief Justice John Marshall administered the oath to John Quincy Adams in the Chamber of the House of Representatives, the room in which he was destined to die 23 years later. As the members of Congress and guests were leaving after the inaugural, the National Intelligencer reported: "No less than four large eagles were seen poising themselves directly over the Capitol for about ten minutes, when one of them apparently larger than the rest, began to descend, and after making a number of circles around the centre dome, arose in graceful spirals. Was their attention attracted by the immense concourse of people about the place, or was the parent eagle...now sent by our guardian spirit with her brood from their mountain eyry to augur continued and increased prosperity to our happy country?"

Unfortunately, the eagles were not a happy omen for the new President. From his first day in office, Adams was opposed by a Congress filled with Jacksonian Democrats. His attempt to institute a program of national public works was stymied by the opposition on the grounds that it encroached on the rights of states. His efforts to get federal funds to establish a national university and a national observatory were thwarted. He did help the Columbian University (later to become George Washington University) get started with a personal loan. Adams had no better success seeking federal money to further research in agriculture or science, or to promote the arts.

Angry but helpless to move the Congress, Adams tried to work off his frustrations by taking long walks before dawn or late at night. During the summer months, he would plunge into the Potomac for an early morning swim. His most demeaning clash with Congress came about when his enemies found out that Adams, who was fond of billiards and chess, had brought the necessary equipment into the White House at his own expense. The President, who particularly enjoyed playing those games with his children, was denounced on the floor of Congress as a corruptor of American youth and accused of running a gaming establishment in the White House. The Adams family and his whole administration were depicted as "desperadoes and debauchees."

Then, as though to add one more cloud to the gathering storm, during the traditional July Fourth White House reception, the President learned of the death of both his father, John Adams, and his father's good friend and rival, Thomas Jefferson. These two men, who had been Founding Fathers and co-signers of the Declaration of Independence, died on the 50th anniversary of that historic event.

When election year 1828 came around, Adams ran for a second term but lost resoundingly to Andrew Jackson. Calhoun was re-elected Vice President.

Throughout Adams' term, his wife, Louisa, had remained a warm and gracious hostess. She brought back a less formal approach to entertaining in the White House than Washington had known under the Monroes, and her dinner parties were noted for their choice foods and rare wines. Even after her husband's defeat, Mrs. Adams refused to be bitter, and, instead, gave one of her biggest and most festive parties, opening up the East Room to dancing for the first time.

The old Indian fighter and military ramrod, President-elect Jackson, never forgave Adams for winning the 1824 election and did not afford him the courtesy of calling on him or communicating directly with him. He did request, through an intermediary, that the Adams family vacate the White House on or before inauguration day so that Jackson could receive his visitors there. In the face of this obvious affront, John Quincy Adams, like his father 28 years before, left Washington on March 4 without seeing his successor sworn into office.

It was warm and spring-like that day in 1829 when Andrew Jackson, Old Hickory to his admirers, took the oath of office on the east portico of the Capitol. Later, he made an imposing figure riding down Pennsylvania Avenue at the head of the post-inaugural parade that included many veterans of the Revolution. Andy Jackson, the first President to be born in a log cabin, was bringing a new style of democracy to the White House. Plans for only a small, simple reception had been made because the President was still in mourning for his wife, Rachel, who had died the previous December 22. Therefore, the White House was completely unprepared for the undisciplined horde of 20,000 people who invaded the grounds and building to welcome the "man of the people." They virtually destroyed thousands of dollars worth of rugs, furniture, china and crystal, and endangered Jackson's safety as they fought to shake his hand. Washington's old guard stood aside and watched and wondered if that scene was a portent of things to come.

From that day until his second term ended eight years later, Jackson was embroiled in social and political controversies such as the nation's capital had not encountered before, or would after. Old Hickory had come to the Presidency convinced that the heart attack that killed his wife had been caused by: (a) slanderous implications made during the campaign which he attributed to Henry Clay and John Quincy Adams; (b) the arrogance of Washington's old-line Southern hostesses who looked down on the less-sophisticated lady with a predilection for smoking a pipe. The basis of the so-called scandal was traced back to 1791, when Jackson and Mrs. Rachel Donelson Robards were married. They believed that Rachel's previous husband had obtained a divorce, when, in fact, he had not. Robards did sue for divorce in 1793, naming Jackson, and won his case. The Jacksons then remarried to legalize their union. After Jackson's election as President, Rachel was reluctantly preparing to accompany him to Washington when, according to an accepted version of the story, she overheard a conversation in which she was described as an adulteress and not her husband's equal socially. Rachel Jackson fell into a state of severe depression which was followed by a fatal heart attack. She was buried the day before Christmas at the Hermitage, the Jackson estate in Nashville, Tennessee, in the white satin gown she had purchased for the inaugural. The funeral was held outdoors with 10,000 mourners in attendance, twice the population of Nashville. Her husband ordered the following epitaph engraved on her tomb: "A being so gentle and virtuous, slander might wound but could not dishonor."

With Rachel gone, the ladies of Washington society found a new target for their disdain. Her name was Peggy O'Neale Timberlake, the widowed daughter of a local tavern and boarding house keeper. Just prior to Jackson's inauguration, Peggy had married John Eaton, a close friend and former colleague of the President when both were Senators from Tennessee. When Jackson appointed Eaton his Secretary of War, the social leaders made it known that the new Mrs. Eaton would not be welcome in their drawing rooms because it was rumored that she had been Eaton's mistress. The President came to Peggy Eaton's defense and categorized the rumor as the same sort of slander that had killed Rachel. When three cabinet members and their wives excluded Mrs. Eaton from their parties, Jackson maneuvered them into resigning. He rebuked Emily Donelson, Rachel's niece and a favorite as his official hostess, for snubbing Mrs. Eaton.

The Eaton affair widened a growing political rift between the President, an advocate of a strong union, and his Vice President, John C. Calhoun, an ardent states rights adherent. Jackson resented the fact that Mrs. Calhoun preferred to remain in South Carolina rather than meet Mrs. Eaton in Washington. Differences between the two men reached a point where Calhoun resigned his office and returned to the Capitol as a Senator from South Carolina, where he felt he was more effective in espousing his beliefs.

The President's staunchest ally at this time was his Secretary of State, Martin Van Buren, a man with larger political aspirations. The controversy proved extremely rewarding for Van Buren, because he became Jackson's Vice President during his second term, and then succeeded him in the White House.

Throughout his two terms, Jackson never hesitated to make changes and use people who endorsed his ideas and philosophy. Cabinet members were particularly vulnerable, and over the eight-year span, Jackson had four Secretaries of State, five Secretaries of the Treasury, three Secretaries of War, three Secretaries of the Navy, three Attorney Generals and two Postmaster Generals.

Jackson's penchant for change extended to the White House, which he had refurbished at great cost after the debacle of his first inauguration. He had the north portico completed, turned the barren East Room into a stately salon, repaired all the old outbuildings and planted magnolia trees close to the southwest corner of the mansion in memory of Rachel. He also had a racing stable built for his thoroughbreds, which were raced on nearby tracks under his nephew's name.

In addition to holding general levees at the White House, the President instituted large-scale, lavish suppers for as many as 1,000 invited guests. They were held in the State Dining Room, where a huge horseshoe table was described as being "covered with every good and glittering thing that French skill could devise . . ."

It was Jackson who ordered Pennsylvania Avenue paved for the first time. And, according to Washington legend, it was during one of his bitter fights with Congress that he insisted that the Treasury building be erected so it would intrude into Pennsylvania Avenue and cut off the view of the Capitol, which it does today. The building was planned by Robert Mills, a former pupil of Hoban's and Latrobe's. Yet, despite his obvious stubbornness and inflexibility, Jackson remained a

hero to the people and undoubtedly could have been elected for a third term, but he declined, refusing to break precedent, much to the relief of his enemies, among them John Quincy Adams. It was Adams, a Harvard alumnus, who wrote to the university on learning that it was about to confer an honorary L.L.D. degree upon Jackson: "As myself an affectionate child of our alma mater, I would not be present to witness her disgrace in conferring the highest literary honors upon a barbarian who could not write a sentence of grammar, and hardly could spell his own name." Jackson was equally unforgiving in his hostility. When asked if he had any regrets about his Presidency, he answered he had just two – he regretted not having shot Henry Clay or hanged John C. Calhoun. Then, after seeing his handpicked successor, Martin Van Buren, safely through the inaugural ceremony on March 4, 1837, Jackson left Washington for his estate in Nashville.

Within days after the new President took office, the country was hit by its first great depression. Bankers blamed Jackson, who had destroyed the United States Bank by refusing to renew its charter. Instead, he had spread public funds among private, so-called "pet-banks" all over the country, and those funds were in jeopardy. Some of that blame spilled over on to Van Buren, and would eventually play an important part in his bid for re-election. For relaxation, Van Buren, a widower, began to give small, elegant dinner parties for a select group of statesmen and politicians, both friends and opponents, and soon had a reputation as a bon vivant.

The Van Buren years were marked by the return of Dolley Madison to live in the former house of her sister, which James had bought and left to her. It was less than a block from the White House. The Washington establishment welcomed her with open arms, and John Quincy Adams noted approvingly: "The depredations of time are not so perceptible in her personal appearance as might have been expected." It didn't take too long before Dolley, concerned about the absence of an official hostess for the White House and the lack of social activity there, arranged for one of her young relatives to meet the President's eldest son. That meeting resulted in marriage between Angelica Singleton and Abraham Van Buren in November, 1838, and Angelica appeared as the radiant hostess at the New Year's reception of 1839. When the government officials and social leaders left the reception that day, they walked down the street to Dolley's house to pay their respects. This custom continued until her death ten years later.

The election campaign of 1840 took some unexpected turns for Van Buren, who ran on the Democratic ticket against the Whig candidate, William Henry Harrison, soldier and politician, whom he had defeated in 1836. This time Van Buren was victimized by the same type of smear tactics he had used against John Quincy Adams when running Old Hickory's campaign. The Whigs determined to depict Van

Buren as a self-indulgent Sybarite who gave extravagant dinners at which gold spoons were used while the rest of the country suffered through the hard times of a depression. It was Representative William Ogle of Pennsylvania, a frequent guest at Van Buren's dinner parties, who made the inflammatory "gold spoons" speech before the House, knowing that the spoons in question were old and gold-plated and had been part of the White House table service since Monroe's time. Ogle went even further, attributing all the major White House purchases for the previous 20 years to Van Buren. Though the accusations were patently false, the Democrats could not devise a strategy to overcome that hate campaign. When they tried to retaliate by picturing Harrison as an uncouth backwoodsman who would be better suited to live in a log cabin with a barrel of hard cider and a small pension, the Whigs made "Log Cabin and Hard Cider" one of their major campaign slogans, along with "Tippecanoe and Tyler too." It mattered not at all that Harrison actually was a Virginia aristocrat whose father, Benjamin, had signed the Declaration of Independence and had been Speaker of the Virginia House of Delegates . . . or that the candidate and his family of ten children had lived in a $20,000 mansion in Vincennes, Indiana, that rivaled the finest homes in Virginia.

From the Hermitage, Andrew Jackson denounced the Whig's campaign tactics as "the vilest system of slander that ever before has existed even in the most corrupt days of ancient Rome." But, it was to no avail. The Whigs swept into office, with Harrison amassing 234 electoral votes (19 states) to Van Buren's 60 electoral votes (7 states).

When Harrison took his oath of office, March 4, 1841, on the east portico of the Capitol, he was, at age 68, the oldest President inaugurated until then. He rode his favorite white horse to the outdoor ceremony, refusing to wear a hat or coat despite the cold, stormy weather. Then, he delivered a long acceptance speech, led the parade back to the White House, and, that evening, attended three inaugural balls. At some point, he caught a severe cold, which worsened into pneumonia by March 27. At 30 minutes past one on Sunday morning, April 4, the ninth President of the United States became the first President to die in office. John Tyler, his running mate, was summoned from his home at Williamsburg, Virginia, to become the first Vice President ever to be elevated to the Presidency because of the death of the Chief Executive. He was sworn in on April 6. The following day, with the city dressed in mourning, President Harrison's body was taken from the East Room, where it had been lying in state, and carried in a two-mile long funeral procession to a public vault before being sent for interment to his Ohio home. By an unprecedented quirk of fate, the White House had been the residence of three Presidents in just over 30 days.

It was not an easy job that John Tyler inherited. The country was still in the throes of economic difficulties, and the Whigs, led by Henry Clay, urged the re-establishment of the United States Bank. But Tyler, coming from the agrarian South, disagreed with the Northern financiers in his party and vetoed two bank bills in succession. The vetoes were so unpopular that public demonstrations in front of the White House burned the President in effigy. Clay tried to cause Tyler's resignation by organizing a mass defection of the cabinet members. This failed when Daniel Webster, then Secretary of State, refused to take part, and Tyler was able to form a new cabinet within 24 hours. He saved his administration but became "the President without a party."

Three years before the Tylers moved into the White House, Letitia Tyler, mother of eight, suffered an almost completely disabling stroke. As the First Lady, she appeared in public only once, to attend the wedding of her daughter in the East Room in January, 1842. She died in September of the same year, the first wife of a president to die while he was in office.

Another event of 1842 was a visit to Washington and the White House by Charles Dickens. The celebrated author approved of the President, saying: "He looked somewhat worn and anxious, and well he might, being at war with everybody . . . but, I thought in his whole carriage and demeanor he became his station singularly well." Mr. Dickens had less flattering things to say about the city, however, which he characterized as "the headquarters of tobacco-tinctured saliva."

"Here is Washington," he wrote, "fresh in my mind and under my eye. It is sometimes called the City of Magnificent Distances, but it might with greater propriety be termed the City of Magnificent Intentions; for it is only on taking a bird's-eye view of it from the top of the Capitol, that one can at all comprehend the vast designs of its projector . . . Spacious avenues that begin in nothing, and lead nowhere; streets, mile-long, that only want houses, roads and inhabitants; public buildings that need but a public to be complete; and ornaments of great thoroughfares, which only lack great thoroughfares to ornament – are its leading features . . ."

Totally aside from the capital, another 1842 event worth noting was the eruption of Mount Saint Helens in the state of Washington, which was something that would not happen again for almost 140 years.

February 28, 1844, proved to be a fateful day – a day that began on a note of light-heartedness and ended with a tragedy. About 400 visitors, including the Chief Executive, cabinet members, diplomats, Congressmen, and their families went aboard the U.S.S. Princeton, the Navy's first propeller-driven warship, for a trial run down the Potomac. In addition to the cruise, a new 10-ton gun called the "Peacemaker" was to be test-fired. Everything went as planned until, on the return trip, the Secretary of the Navy ordered that the

"Peacemaker" be tested once more. When the gun was discharged, it exploded and burst at the breech, killing several people and wounding many others. Among the dead were the Secretary of the Navy, the Secretary of State and a former New York state senator named David Gardiner, the owner of Gardiners Island off the coast of Long Island.

At the time of the accident, President Tyler was on a lower deck conversing with some guests, among them Julia Gardiner, the beautiful young daughter of the man who was killed. Another guest was Dolley Madison, who proved to be a very capable nurse as she pitched in to help the wounded.

After the victims were given a state funeral, the President consoled Miss Gardiner and began a courtship that culminated in their marriage that June. He was 54 at the time, and she was 24.

One of Tyler's long-frustrated Presidential ambitions was the annexation of Texas. Unable to muster enough support on his own, he agreed to a compromise that meant giving up his candidacy in 1844 and throwing his support to the pro-Texas Democrat James K. Polk of Tennessee. The strategy worked, and Polk won the election, beating Henry Clay, the anti-Texas Whig nominee. Assured now that her husband's goal would be reached, Julia Tyler gave a huge ball in the White House. When Tyler saw the 2,000 guests on hand, he said jokingly: "They cannot now say I am a President without a party."

On March 1, Tyler signed a joint resolution of Congress to annex Texas, and three days later left Washington.

Once again, inclement weather dampened the March 4, 1845, ceremonies held outdoors on the Capitol's east portico. But with a doggedness that would be evident throughout his term, James K. Polk, the eleventh President, read his inaugural address to what John Quincy Adams was overheard describing as "a large assemblage of umbrellas."

For James and Sarah Polk, it was a day to be savored because not many months before, they were virtually unknown outside of limited political circles. He had been a Congressman from Tennessee, Speaker of the United States House of Representatives and Governor of Tennessee, but his name carried nowhere near the import or charisma of the man he eventually defeated, Henry Clay. In May, 1844, when Polk attended the Democratic convention in Baltimore, he was seeking the Vice Presidential nomination. With the convention deadlocked over its choice for standard bearer, Polk's name was entered as a compromise candidate on the eighth ballot. On the next ballot, the convention stampeded for Polk, and he was nominated unanimously. The news of his nomination was flashed from Odd Fellows' Hall Baltimore, to Washington via telegraph, the first time that instrument was used in politics.

The Washington National Intelligencer reported: "During the whole day a crowd of persons, including a number of Members of Congress, were in attendance at the Capitol to receive the reports by telegraph of news from Baltimore, which were made at successive intervals with striking dispatch and accuracy, and were received by the auditors, as the responses of the ancient Oracle may be supposed to have been ... Whatever variety of impression the news made upon the auditory, however, there was but one sentiment concerning the telegraph itself, which was that of mingled delight and wonder."

Twenty minutes after Polk had been nominated, the following telegram was sent to the convention from Washington: "The Democratic members of Congress to their Democratic brethren in convention assembled. Three cheers for James K. Polk."

When the Whigs, who were running Henry Clay, and most of the American public asked, "Who is James K. Polk?", the Democrats, with the endorsement of Andrew Jackson, replied, "Young Hickory." The voters responded by electing their first "Dark Horse" and thwarting Clay's bid for the highest office again.

With the arrival of the Polks at the White House, social activities took on a much more staid and somber air, because Sarah Polk, a devout Presbyterian, did not approve of dancing, alcoholic beverages of any kind, card playing or anything even slightly frivolous. The Polks received guests informally in the parlor two nights a week, among them Dolley Madison. Though she knew that Dolley indulged in many of the pastimes of which she disapproved, including taking snuff, Sarah Polk always accorded her the highest honors at White House receptions. The Polks did add one light touch to their stay in the White House – they had gas illumination installed.

On the political front, Polk saw Texas safely admitted to the union as the 28th state in December, 1845, and then began looking for ways of furthering U.S. expansion to the Pacific Ocean. That opportunity came when the United States and Mexico went to war in May, 1846, over a dispute concerning the exact location of the southern boundary of Texas. When Mexico City fell to General Winfield Scott in September, 1847, Mexico agreed to the Treaty of Guadalupe Hidalgo which established the Rio Grande River as the international border. It also ceded to the United States for $15,000,000, approximately 525,000 square miles of territory that would become the states of California, Nevada and Utah, most of Arizona and New Mexico and parts of Colorado and Wyoming. An interesting footnote to the war was that it gave combat experience to a group of young West Point-trained Army officers, who would put it to use a dozen years later. Among them were Ulysses S. Grant, William T. Sherman, Robert E. Lee and Thomas (Stonewall) Jackson.

To commemorate the victory and the expansion of the country to the Pacific Ocean, the President had the treaty delivered to him on July 4, 1848. On the same day, he laid the cornerstone of the Washington Monument, with Dolley Madison and Mrs. Alexander Hamilton as honored guests. Dolley, incidentally, had recently been saved from severe financial straits when Congress voted an appropriation of $25,000 to buy her husband's personal and public papers.

Other noteworthy occurrences of that year were: the discovery of gold in California by James W. Marshall; the demise of John Quincy Adams on the floor of the House Chamber after almost 17 years as a Congressman from Massachusetts; a woman's rights convention, held at Seneca Falls, New York; the first election to be held under the law that set the first Tuesday after the first Monday in November of every even-numbered year for federal balloting in every state.

When the Presidential nominating conventions were held that year, Polk, true to the pledge he had made on taking office, declined to run for re-election and also refused to take an active part in the campaign. As a result, the election went to the Whigs, who had run General Zachary Taylor, a hero of the Mexican War. The following February, the Polks held their final White House reception, which, coincidentally, became the last one for the venerable Mrs. Madison. But even at age 82, Dolley appeared in a white satin gown, cut decolette, with her usual turban of the same material wrapped around her head.

On Inaugural day, Monday, March 5, President Polk rode to Capitol Hill with President-elect Taylor and returned with him to the White House after the ceremony. That night, Polk wrote in his diary: "I feel exceedingly relieved that I am now free from all public cares. I am sure I shall be a happier man in my retirement than I have been the four years I have filled the highest office..."

Polk had little time to enjoy his retirement, however. He died on June 15, at his home, Polk Place, in the heart of Nashville. Less than one month later, on July 12, Mrs. James (Dolley) Madison passed away, and Washington said its farewells at funeral services fit for a President.

General Zachary Taylor was 64 years old when he took the oath of office, and, according to his predecessor's assessment of him, he was "a well-meaning old man, uneducated, exceedingly ignorant of public affairs, and, I should judge, of very ordinary capacity." His wife, Margaret, descended from leading families of Maryland and Virginia, was not in good health and strongly opposed her husband's candidacy because of the strain it might impose on his health. But the General persevered, and when he was elected, Mrs. Taylor reluctantly moved to the White House, where she became a social recluse, seeing only family and very close friends.

Among them was Senator Jefferson Davis, a former son-in-law, whose first wife, Sarah Knox Taylor, had died of typhoid fever three months after their marriage. Mrs. Betty Bliss, another Taylor daughter, took over the role of official hostess.

A special White House favorite was Old Whitey, the war horse which had carried Taylor through many campaigns. Given the run of the mansion's grounds, Old Whitey could frequently be seen grazing contentedly on the White House lawn.

An assertive leader on the battlefield, but basically an unpretentious and politically unsophisticated man, the President inherited an unresolved and volatile problem that could be likened to a malignancy. Though it existed since the beginning of the Union, it had been suppressed, kept in a state of remission for many years as the result of various legislative compromises. But now, with the acquisition of the Mexican territories, California in particular, it was threatening to erupt and destroy the Union. The name of the problem: slavery.

Up to this point, the pro-slavery forces of the South and the anti-slavery proponents of the North had been appeased by the compromise system of admitting states to the Union in pairs, one for each side. There were now 15 slave states and 15 free states. California, with a prohibition against slavery in its constitution, wanted admission as a free state, which would upset the balance in favor of the North. For nine months, both Houses of Congress debated the issue led by those two perennial and aged opponents, South Carolina's John C. Calhoun and Massachusetts' Daniel Webster. Out of that stalemate, Henry Clay produced one of his famous compromises, said to have been authored by Stephen A. Douglas, wherein four of five separate acts would: (1) admit California as a free state; (2) permit the territories of New Mexico and Utah to have self-determination as to slavery; (3) prohibit the slave trade in the District of Columbia; (4) strengthen the enforcement of the Fugitive Slave Act of 1793. The fifth act concerned the assumption of a $10,000,000 debt incurred by Texas when it was a republic.

Zach Taylor was a slave-owning Southerner, but he went on record as saying: "Attachment to the Union of the States should be habitually fostered in every American heart. Dissolution would be the greatest calamity." He also believed that "Disunion is treason." He never got the chance to enforce his views, because on July 9, 1850, five days after attending a big Independence Day celebration at the site of the Washington Monument, he died in the White House. Cause of death: there are three versions – an attack of cholera, typhoid fever or coronary thrombosis. To the accompaniment of muted funeral music and the ritual booming of heavy guns, Old Whitey followed his master's coffin in this final procession.

If Taylor could be called "Old Rough and Ready," his Vice President and successor to the White House, Millard Fillmore, presented a completely opposite image. Handsome and courtly, the new Chief Executive – he was sworn in on July 10 – was born on the New York State frontier of hard-working farm folks. Largely self-taught until he was a late teenager, he came under the tutelage of Miss Abigail Powers, whom he later married after he was admitted to the bar. Though Taylor and he ran on the Whig ticket, they actually represented two different factions within the party. Thus, when Taylor died, his entire cabinet resigned and left town. They were followers of the so-called "Radical" Whigs, and they opposed the Fugitive Slave Act. Fillmore replaced them with more conservative "Silver Grays," whose beliefs were closer akin to Daniel Webster, the man who became Secretary of State.

When Congress passed the amended Fugitive Slave Law in September, Fillmore was confronted with an onerous decision. If he did not sign the bill, he was faced with the very real threat of the South seceding. If he did sign the bill, he knew he would destroy his political career in the North and probably the Whig party too. Fillmore chose to sign the bill, and by doing so, he is credited with delaying the outbreak of the Civil War by ten years.

While the legislators were discussing the potential break-up of the Union, they were complaining about their crowded quarters in the Capitol at the same time. So, 21 years after the building had been completed according to Thornton's plans, Congress appropriated funds to enlarge the structure. President Fillmore appointed Thomas U. Walter as the Architect of the Capitol Extension, a post he held from 1851 until 1865. The cornerstone for the extension of the south wing was laid on July 4. The House met in its new Chamber in December, 1857. The new Senate Chamber was ready in January, 1859.

Meanwhile, Mrs. Fillmore, a prolific reader and ardent booklover, secured some Congressional funds to install a library in the White House. On the whole, the social life of the Fillmores was quiet and relatively unglamorous. Mrs. Fillmore was not in robust health, so her activity was kept down to a reception each Tuesday morning and a levee each Friday evening when Congress was in session, along with an occasional dinner.

Knowing he had little chance to win re-election, Fillmore sent a letter to the Whig convention in 1852 withdrawing his name from consideration. The delegates refused to accept his withdrawal and included him on the ballot. It took 53 ballots to nominate Mexican war veteran and hero, General Winfield Scott. Soon after the close of the convention, Henry Clay died, never having achieved his most cherished and long-denied ambition, the Presidency. And that other old stalwart, Daniel Webster, died at the end of the campaign.

The Democrats also nominated a dark horse, Franklin Pierce, a native of New Hampshire, who ran away with the election, gaining 85 percent of the electoral votes.

A pall seemed to hang over President Pierce's term from the blustery, snowy day of his inauguration in 1853 until he was rejected by his own party for renomination three years later. More than 80,000 braved the cold to witness the Presidential oath taking and hear Pierce become the only Chief Executive to say, "I do solemnly affirm," instead of "I do solemnly swear." But only about 15,000 remained to see him deliver his speech as an oration instead of reading it, another first.

Jane Pierce did not attend her husband's inauguration because the Pierces were still in deep mourning over the loss of their third and last surviving young son in a recent railroad wreck from which the adults emerged unhurt. There were no inaugural balls that year in deference to the First Family's bereavement.

Later in the month, Mrs. Abigail Fillmore died, reportedly from a severe chill she contracted during the ceremony at the Capitol. And William Rufus DeVan King, the Vice President, died at his Alabama home on April 17, never having assumed his duties in Washington. King had taken his oath of office from the United States Consul at Havana, Cuba, where he was recuperating from an illness.

Aside from the mandatory receptions and state dinners, the Pierces did not indulge in extensive entertaining. Jane Pierce suffered from tuberculosis and tired very quickly, and the President was a member of the Temperance Society. So the social scene shifted from the White House to the home of Secretary of War Jefferson Davis and his wife. One of the notable events at the Executive Mansion was the installation of the first furnace, after which the building was painted inside and out. The President started one other beautification project that can still be seen and enjoyed today. He approved the commissioning of Constantino Brumidi to decorate the interior of the Capitol.

Brumidi, an Italian artist with an outstanding reputation, had come to the United States in 1852, to escape political persecution at home. His primary ambition, he said, was "to make beautiful the Capitol of the one country on earth in which there is liberty." He got his wish two years later, and for the next 25 years, he devoted himself to this labor of love which he always signed "C. Brumidi, artist. Citizen of the U.S." Brumidi died in poverty in 1879 and was buried in an unmarked grave. Seventy years later, the 81st Congress voted to erect a suitable monument to the man who had made such an unselfish and invaluable contribution to the Capitol.

Pierce's political popularity in the North plunged when he

championed the Kansas-Nebraska Bill which allowed those territories to become states under self-determination as to slavery. Nebraska had determined to be free, so the South was trying to pressure Kansas into being a slave state despite the fact that the Missouri Compromise of 1820 barred slave states north of the 36°31' parallel. Pierce further alienated his supporters by personally taking charge of the return of a slave under the Fugitive Slave Act.

Though he knew his chances for renomination were slim, Pierce allowed his name to be presented when the Democrats convened at Cincinnati, Ohio, in June, 1856. It took 17 ballots before the convention went unanimously for James Buchanan of Pennsylvania.

James Buchanan, former Congressman, cabinet member, envoy to Russia and Great Britain, was a tall, distinguished-looking bachelor of 65 when he led the Democrats to victory in 1856 over John Charles Fremont, candidate of the fledgling Republican party. His inauguration on March 4, 1857, signalled the return of more exciting days to the White House. Following the inaugural ceremony on the east portico of the Capitol, great crowds lined Pennsylvania Avenue to cheer for a huge parade featuring numerous floats that depicted various historical scenes. That evening, in a building specially constructed at the cost of $15,000, approximately 6,000 attended the inaugural ball. They danced to the music of a 40-piece orchestra, and consumed the following items at supper: 400 gallons of oysters, 60 saddles of mutton, 4 saddles of venison, 125 tongues, 75 hams, 500 quarts of chicken salad, 500 quarts of jellies, 1200 quarts of ice cream, and a cake four feet high. The cost of the wine alone was over $3,000.

The White House once again became the focal point for elegant parties and receptions, with Harriet Lane, the President's young niece and legal ward, presiding and setting the new trends in fashion. European royalty, including the Prince of Wales, later King Edward VII, and the Prince de Joinville, third son of Louis Philippe of France, visited the newly repaired and refurnished old mansion. Because Buchanan felt these visits were more of a personal nature than an affair of state, he paid all expenses for them out of his own pocket. And as an indication of the friendship that had developed between them when he was representing the United States at the British court, the President and Queen Victoria exchanged warmest greetings via the recently completed Atlantic cable.

While the White House was enjoying a physical and social rejuvenation, the political situation between the North and South was deteriorating rapidly. Two days after Buchanan's inauguration, Roger Taney, Chief Justice of the United States Supreme Court, announced what has come to be known as the Dred Scott decision. The Court declared the Missouri Compromise to be unconstitutional. It said that Congress had no right to prohibit slavery in the territories. And further, it maintained that Dred Scott, a slave who was suing for his freedom on the basis of having been taken to live in the free state of Illinois and the free territories of Minnesota and Wisconsin and then returned to the slave state of Missouri, was not free. The court held that a Negro "whose ancestors were . . . sold as slaves" was not entitled to the rights of a Federal citizen and therefore had no standing in court.

The President urged all good citizens to abide by the Dred Scott decision, but Senator Stephen A. Douglas, the "Little Giant" of Illinois, became the very vocal leader of the opposition within the Democratic party. This disagreement split the Democratic party wide open. When it held its Presidential convention at Charleston, South Carolina, in April of 1860, the delegates from the cotton states walked out before a platform could be adopted or a candidate nominated. The convention met again in Baltimore that June and nominated Stephen Douglas. The Southern delegates walked out again, held their own convention that same day and nominated John C. Breckinridge of Kentucky.

The Republicans had already met in Chicago the previous month and nominated Abraham Lincoln of Illinois on the third ballot. Lincoln won a resounding victory in November with almost 60 percent of the electoral votes, with Breckinridge a distant second and Douglas completely out of contention. Immediately after the election, South Carolina, which had been threatening to secede since Jackson's Presidency, finally made good that threat. Six more Southern states followed that lead soon after.

In a last ditch effort to save the Union, Virginia sent former President John Tyler to Washington to propose to Buchanan that a Peace Convention be held there. The President concurred, and throughout the month of February, 1861, delegates from the North and South tried to come to some agreement, but to no avail. Meanwhile, on February 18, Jefferson Davis was chosen President of the Confederate States of America.

Two weeks later, a thoroughly disheartened but relieved James Buchanan rode in the same carriage with the President-elect to the inaugural despite the known threat of an assassination attempt on Lincoln's life. Buchanan is reported to have said to the incoming President when they met at the White House: "If you are as happy, my dear sir, on entering this house as I am on leaving it and returning home, you are the happiest man on earth."

Few heads of state have been beset by more difficult and discouraging circumstances than Abraham Lincoln even before he took the oath of office on March 4, 1861. Because of threats to his life – one such plot was thwarted by Allen Pinkerton, a detective assigned to guard Lincoln while he was en route to Washington from Springfield, Illinois for the inauguration – his honor escort to and from the Capitol was in reality a military bodyguard.

The antagonism between North and South was on the verge of breaking out into open warfare. The Southern aristocracy, that had dominated the Washington social scene from its earliest days, was unbashedly hostile to the incoming Republican administration that threatened to destroy its way of life, not only in the capital but throughout the South. And to add another worry to his load, the President's wife, Mary Todd Lincoln, a Southern lady schooled in all the accepted social graces, alternated between emotional outbursts and extravagant shopping sprees for clothes in her frustration at being snubbed by the Southern elite.

Then, on April 12, a blow was struck. The Governer of secessionist South Carolina had demanded that the U.S. Army surrender Fort Sumter, located in Charleston Harbor, to Confederate troops. When the fort's commander, Major Robert Anderson, refused to comply, Confederate guns opened fire. Federal troops held out under bombardment for 34 hours before Anderson capitulated and abandoned the site. Miraculously, not a man was killed by the shelling. Now, there was no turning back, however; the lines were drawn, the battle joined.

President Lincoln issued a call for 75,000 volunteers and Robert E. Lee was offered command of the Union forces. He declined, preferring to serve his native state, Virginia. Soon thereafter, his wife, the only surviving child of George Washington Parke Custis, grandson of Martha Washington, left her ancestral home, Arlington, and fled to the South. The Custis-Lee estate became the first enemy property seized because its hilltop acres were strategically important to the defense of the city.

Divided loyalties brought anguish to many families as it did to Mary Todd Lincoln. Among the 16 children sired by her twice-married father, she had a full brother, three half-brothers plus three brothers-in-law in the Confederate ranks. Because of the number of her relatives who favored the South, Mrs. Lincoln's own sympathies became the subject of a vicious rumor. It reached the point where a Senatorial Committee on the Conduct of the War held a special meeting to weigh the validity of the gossip. The rumor was abruptly and firmly squelched when the President appeared unannounced before the committee and stated: "I, Abraham Lincoln, President of the United States, appear of my own volition before this committee of the Senate to say that I, of my own knowledge, know that it is untrue that any of my family hold treasonable communication (relations) with the enemy."

Soon after the call to arms, Washington became a huge base camp, and its usual population of 70,000 more than doubled as troops and supplies moved to the battle areas and the wounded returned later to the many hospitals that had sprung up. Roadways were jammed with military traffic, and blue uniforms could be seen everywhere. The grounds around the Washington Monument became cattle pens for slaughtering beef, while other open spaces were converted into corrals for the cavalry and quartermaster horses. At one point, the Capitol itself was used as a barracks for 3,000 Union soldiers. It was later set up temporarily as a hospital. While this activity was going on in and around the building, renovation work on the Capitol continued, with special attention to the raising of a new, larger cast-iron dome that Architect Walter had designed to replace Bulfinch's smaller, copper-sheathed dome. This new dome, painted white and topped by the now-famous statue of Freedom, was completed, inside and out, by the end of 1865. The President was extremely pleased to see the work proceed despite the disruptions of war, because, as he is reported to have said, "If the world sees this Capitol going on, they will know that we intend the Union shall go on."

The city itself was surrounded by impressive earthworks that had been organized by General George B. McClellan. Unfortunately, General McClellan was better at organizing than fighting, which seemed to be the case with many early Union commanders. In desperation, the President himself took command of the Army and Navy and relieved several generals until he found a satisfactory one serving in the Army of the West. His name: Ulysses S. Grant.

Union morale sagged because of several costly defeats at the hands of Robert E. Lee, and Lincoln knew he had to take some dramatic action to bolster the spirits in the North. He found the right tonic when he abolished slavery in the District of Columbia in April, 1862, and then issued a preliminary proclamation in September, announcing the freeing of all slaves on January 1, 1863.

Morale at the White House also could have used a boost, particularly Mrs. Lincoln's. Earlier in the year, she had decided to dispense with her social obligations by having one big reception instead of numerous state dinners and smaller functions. Fearing that the affair would be overcrowded, she had invitations sent to a limited guest list, which immediately evoked angry protests from those who felt they should have been included. To soothe those injured egos, the guest list was expanded, which resulted in the affair becoming, as one attendee said, "no ball, no party, nothing but a jam."

But while the Marine Band played on, the two young Lincoln sons, Willie and Tad, were very ill in their beds upstairs. The Lincolns proposed postponing the party, but their doctor reassured them that there was nothing to worry about. He was wrong. Though Tad did improve and recovered, Willie died of typhoid fever. He was eleven years old. Mrs. Lincoln was so grief-stricken she could not attend the funeral. She never again walked into the room in which Willie died, and banned all flowers from the White House because Willie had loved them. She stopped the Marine Band from playing summer concerts on the White House lawn because she could not abide the sound of happy music.

January 1, 1863. After shaking hands all day at the traditional White House New Year's Day reception, Abraham Lincoln signed his name to the Emancipation Proclamation. That document, like a harbinger of better times to come for the North, became the prelude to a series of Union victories that year and the next. And those victories brought Lincoln the renomination at the Republican convention held in Baltimore in June, 1864. They also brought him a total triumph over his Democratic opponent, George McClellan, with 90 percent of the electoral votes.

Mr. Lincoln's popularity did not extend to his wife, whose public behavior continued to provoke criticism. One lady newspaper reporter wrote: "While her sister-women scraped lint, sewed bandages and put on nurses' caps, and gave their all to country and to death, the wife of the President spent the time in rolling to and from Washington and New York, intent on extravagant purchases for herself and the White House … Every railroad train that entered the city bore fresh troops to the Nation's rescue, and fresh mourners seeking their dead … Through it all, Mrs. Lincoln 'shopped.'"

Lincoln's second inaugural, during which he delivered his masterful and conciliatory address that began: "With malice towards none, with charity for all, with firmness in the right . . .," was marred by the slightly tipsy behavior of his Vice President, Andrew Johnson. Johnson, a non-drinker and still weak from typhoid fever, had drunk some liquor for medicinal purposes before the ceremony, which caused him to be embarrassingly unsteady and a little incoherent when he tried to speak.

More than 15,000 people crowded into the White House inaugural reception that Saturday night, March 4, 1865, unaware that they were attending the last great affair for the incumbents. The war was winding down, and the First Family took a trip aboard the River Queen to visit General Grant's headquarters at City Point, Virginia. By the time the boat arrived at its destination, Richmond had fallen. The President went ashore and walked into the still-burning city to Jefferson Davis' mansion to personally offer the Confederate President an honorable peace, but Davis had already fled. The war officially ended on April 9, with Lee's surrender to Grant at Appomattox Courthouse, Virginia.

The North erupted into a round of festivities to welcome the return of peace, but all the celebrations came to a sudden and shattering halt just five days later. On the night of Good Friday, April 14, the President was assassinated, shot in the head by actor John Wilkes Booth as he sat in his box at Ford's Theatre, watching Laura Keene in the play, "Our American Cousin." At the same time, other conspirators attacked Secretary of State William Seward at his home, and he barely escaped with his life.

Lincoln was carried across the street to a boarding house, where he died a little after seven o'clock the following morning. His body lay in state at the White House and then the Capitol Rotunda until April 20. The next day, it was placed aboard a train for the trip to its final resting place in Springfield, Illinois, a trip that took 12 days to complete because the train made numerous stops along the route to allow people to pay their last respects.

For five weeks after her husband's death, Mrs. Lincoln closeted herself in an upstairs room in the White House, while below, scavengers and souvenir hunters pillaged the lower floor. When at last she left the White House for Chicago, President Johnson and his family moved into the ravaged mansion.

From the moment he took the oath of office in a small, quiet ceremony in his suite at the Kirkwood House in Washington on the morning of April 15, Andrew Johnson became the target of more undeserved abuse and acrimonious treatment than any Chief Executive before or after him. A man of modest means and modest pretensions, he had struggled up the political ladder in Tennessee despite his humble origin – he had been an unschooled tailor who was taught to write when he was 17 by his teenage bride, the daughter of a shoemaker. He was Lincoln's choice for running mate in the 1864 election and not the choice of the radical Northerners in the Republican party who considered him a Southern Democrat. Some of them went so far as to insinuate that the then Vice President was involved in the Southern conspiracy that killed Lincoln, completely ignoring the fact that because of Johnson's leadership East Tennessee had sent 40,000 men to fight for the Union, including members of his immediate family.

The irrevocable split between the President and the radical Republicans concerned the administration's Reconstruction policy for the South. Johnson favored Lincoln's more lenient philosophy expressed in his second inaugural address, but the radicals in Congress demanded a more punitive policy. So, when Congress voted an excessive measure into law, Johnson vetoed it, and Congress overrode the veto. Then, knowing Johnson wanted to dismiss his Secretary of War, Edwin M. Stanton, one of the radical leaders, Congress passed the Tenure of Office Bill. It decreed that the President had no right to dismiss any appointee who had to be ratified by the Senate. To bring matters to a head, Johnson dismissed Stanton during a Congressional recess on January, 1867, and appointed General Grant to the post. When Congress returned, the Senate voted to disapprove the dismissal, Grant returned to his Army duties and Stanton took his office again. When Johnson tried to remove him once more, Stanton barricaded himself in his office and lived there from February until May.

Now the issue became a test case. The Senate adopted a resolution declaring the President did not have the authority to remove the cabinet member. The House voted unanimously to impeach Johnson. According to Constitutional procedure, the case went to trial in the Senate, with Chief Justice Salmon P. Chase presiding, and lasted from March 13, 1868, to May 26. The final vote: 35 for conviction, 19 for acquittal. As the two-thirds vote necessary for conviction fell one vote short – Johnson was acquitted.

If Johnson wanted more convincing vindication, he received it seven years later when, as a newly-elected Senator, he took his oath of office and his seat in the Senate Chamber to thunderous applause from the floor and packed galleries.

The 1868 election swept the Republican standard bearer, Ulysses S. Grant, into office with almost 73 percent of the electoral vote. He was the first of three Civil War generals who would keep the Presidency under Republican control.

The most notable absentee at Grant's inauguration was outgoing President Andrew Johnson, who, still resentful of Grant's actions during the Stanton affair, refused to attend. The inaugural ceremony was followed by a very impressive military parade, with eight full divisions of troops participating.

When General Grant took office, both the White House and the city of Washington were in dire need of extensive improvements. Mrs. Julia Grant undertook the task of renovating the Executive Mansion, which she accomplished with such dispatch that it was ready shortly for her weekly receptions and more elaborate entertainments. The President, in turn, became a driving force in seeing that the city was raised from its primitive post-war state to a level more suited to the nation's capital. But before any work could be started Congress placed the area completely under its control for the first time. From 1802 right up to this time, Washington was self-governing under a charter that provided for an elective mayor and a council chosen by property holders. The city maintained services for its residents through the collection of local taxes, but it usually ran into debt just trying to keep up the public works and facilities, much less improving them.

To resolve this problem, Congress merged Georgetown and the rest of the 69-mile District into a Territory. (The land originally ceded for the District by Virginia had been returned to that state in 1846.) It decreed that this Territory would be ruled by a Presidentially-appointed governor and an 11-man council, and a popularly-elected 22-member House of Delegates. In addition, a Board of Public Works, also named by the President, would be responsible for improving the city.

One of the board members was a young, dynamic contractor-businessman named Alexander R. Shepherd, who had dreamed of making Washington into a modern city. Through his efforts, the city embarked on a major program of street grading and paving, sewer construction and tree planting (70,000 saplings) that created hundreds of much-needed jobs. It changed the city's look from that of a frontier village, but it also ran the city's debt up to $20,000,000. Grant was so impressed with the progress that he made Shepherd Governor of the Territory. But then the unexpected happened – the Depression of 1873 struck, and Shepherd could not raise any more money. Faced with the prospect of a bankrupt capital, Congress stepped in again to bail out the city and reorganize the government once more. The new system called for three Presidentially-named commissioners – one always to be an Army Engineer who would oversee physical development – to divide most of the District's governmental functions among them. Other administrative bodies, including the Health Department and the Board of Education, were also to be appointed. Local residents lost their right to vote either for city officials or federal officeholders. In return, Congress promised to pay for half of the annual operating budget. The system remained in effect until the 1960s.

Along with the physical and political changes, another change took place in post-war Washington that was to have an even more lasting and oppressive impact. It was a population change. In 1800, when Washington was no more than an under-developed Southern village, it became the national capital of a country founded on the precepts of "liberty and justice for all." Its population then numbered a little more than 3,000 people, including over 600 slaves and 100 or so freed blacks. Through the years, two diametrically opposed standards of life developed that were continually in conflict. On the one hand, the Washington slave traffic supplying Southern plantation owners flourished for the next 50 years, with slave ships bringing their human cargo right up the Potomac to the capital for sale at local auctions. At the same time, Washington became an important station in the "underground railroad," the network established by Northern Abolitionists who trafficked in assisting runaway slaves to freedom. Washington also became a magnet for slaves who had been set free by their owners, even though the city offered them very little in the way of civil rights or employment opportunities.

The Compromise of 1850 brought an end to the slave trade in the District, and the Emancipation Proclamation ended slavery in the country. Many freed blacks, with no place else to go, flocked to Washington looking for comfort and aid from the government. Over 1,500 ex-slaves were housed and fed at Freedmen's Village on Robert E. Lee's old estate, now

Arlington Cemetery. Congress created the Freedmen's Bureau to promote new employment opportunities and better social conditions. Blacks were enfranchised, and, soon after, elected a number of their own representatives to the city council. City ordinances were passed prohibiting racial discrimination in public places. Some jobs in the government opened up to blacks. The city directory discontinued using the letter "c" to denote colored residents. In 1867, Howard University was founded, bearing the name of Civil War General Oliver Otis Howard, who headed the Freedmen's Bureau.

But all the idealistic hopes and promises of those early post-war years were virtually destroyed a short time later by two events, the revocation of home rule and the reappearance of Southern white supremacists in Congress and in the power elite of the city. Now, without the vote to give them a voice in local affairs, without property to give them adequate housing, and without businesses to give them employment opportunities, the blacks were shunted into ghetto-like, backwater alleys with little or no chance to improve their lot. Racists fomented discrimination again, and turned Washington into a "Jim Crow" city.

In addition to the happenings in Washington, Grant's two terms included a major financial scandal, the start of the transcontinental railroad, the invention of the telephone, and the annihilation of General Custer by Chief Sitting Bull at Little Big Horn.

When the mantle of succession passed to Rutherford B. Hayes in 1876, it did not pass easily. Hayes, the Republican, lost the popular vote to Democrat Samuel J. Tilden by almost 300,000, but claimed to have won the electoral vote, 185-184. The issue was not settled until the night before the scheduled inauguration when a commission of 15 voted 8-7 to give the election to Hayes. The next four years in the White House were not especially distinguished, although the Hayes did introduce the first bathrooms, installed the first telephone and telegraph and opened the grounds for the annual Easter Egg Roll.

When Hayes decided not to run for re-election in 1880, the Republican choice, on the 36th ballot, was James A. Garfield. As President, Garfield barely had time to complete four months in office before he was shot and fatally wounded on July 3 at the Washington railroad station by Charles Guiteau, a disappointed office seeker. Garfield, the second President to be assassinated, lingered until September 19, 1881. His assassin was tried, convicted and hanged the following June.

Vice President Chester Alan Arthur, a recent widower, was sworn in as the 21st President at his home in New York on September 20, and again two days later in the Vice President's room at the Capitol. This marked the second time in American history that there were three Presidents in one year.

On viewing the interior of the Executive Mansion, the new tenant said, "I will not live in a house looking this way," and moved into the Capitol Hill home of a friend for three months while the White House was redecorated by designer and artist Louis Comfort Tiffany. It took 24 wagonloads to clear out the old contents, all to be sold at public auction. Among the changes made at the White House were the installation of the first elevator, two baths and a French chef.

When Arthur first took office he met hostility and resentment from his own party members as well as from the opposition, but he proved to be such an able administrator and politician that disparagement soon turned to praise. For example, Mark Twain commented: "I am but one in 55,000,000; still in the opinion of this one-fifty-five millionth of the country's population, it would be hard to better President Arthur's Administration."

Arthur's vulnerable spot was his passion for clothes as well as his expensive taste in wine and food. As time for the 1884 nominating convention neared, Arthur's enemies began spreading false rumors that he was spending public funds to support his elegant dress and life style. Just as Martin Van Buren had been victimized almost fifty years earlier by spurious stories about using gold spoons in the White House, Arthur was said to have been "defeated by his trousers." He lost the nomination to James G. Blaine.

As one of his last official acts, Arthur dedicated the recently-finished Washington Monument on February 21, 1885, more than 36 years after the cornerstone was laid. And for his final official gesture, he signed an act giving former President Grant a general's full commission for life, to prevent Grant from being ruined financially by the bankruptcy of his Wall Street Company.

After a 24-year tenancy, the Republican grip on the White House was broken when Democrat Grover Cleveland outpolled James G. Blaine in both the popular and electoral vote. He and James Buchanan were the only bachelors elected President and like Buchanan, Cleveland also had a young ward. She was Miss Frances Folsom, daughter of Cleveland's deceased law partner, and the President married her the year after taking office. It was the only marriage of a President ever to take place in the White House. She was 21 and he 49.

The White House at this time was in such need of repairs that Cleveland bought a private home where the First Family then lived for most of his term. The Clevelands used the Executive Mansion as a residence only during the social season when they had to entertain.

After a relatively uneventful term – one of the bright spots was the dedication of the Statue of Liberty in New York harbor in 1886 – Cleveland was nominated by acclamation on the first ballot at the Democratic convention in 1888. His re-election seemed assured until the Republicans began a vigorous two-pronged smear campaign. On the economic front, they attacked Cleveland as being pro-British industry and anti-American because he wanted to lower the tariffs. On the home front, they accused him of mistreating his young wife and causing her to flee in the middle of the night. All of the allegations were completely unfounded, but despite the most vehement denials, the Republican candidate, Benjamin Harrison, grandson of William Henry Harrison, won the election. Harrison actually lost the popular vote by 100,000 but won 58 percent of the electoral votes.

The Harrison years in the White House saw the installation of electricity and the start of Mrs. Harrison's collection of china from past Presidencies, a tradition that has been continued. More states (6) were admitted into the Union during this administration than any other. And for the first time in U.S. history, Congressional appropriations reached a billion dollars.

The election of 1892 saw Grover Cleveland reclaiming the White House from Harrison. The other half of the winning ticket was Adlai Ewing Stevenson, whose son would be an unsuccessful Presidential candidate 60 years later. When the Clevelands returned, they brought with them an infant daughter, and a second daughter was born in the White House in September, 1893, the only child of a President to claim that distinction. But along with the happy event that year came two crises: the country was struck by a financial panic, and the President discovered he had a cancer on the roof of his mouth. Rather than add to the public's problems, Cleveland went aboard a friend's yacht in New York on June 26, ostensibly for a short vacation cruise. He was secretly operated on by a three-man surgical team on July 1, and his entire left upper jaw removed. Five days later, he went ashore at his summer home in Buzzards Bay, Cape Cod. He underwent a second operation later that month and then was fitted with an artifical jaw of vulcanized rubber. The appliance changed his appearance so little that he could address Congress that fall without attracting any undue attention. Cleveland survived for 15 years after those secret operations, and when he died it was because of a gastrointestinal ailment.

At the next nominating convention, William Jennings Bryan won the Democratic candidacy and the right to contest Republican William McKinley for the election of 1896. When the ballots were counted, McKinley had won by substantial margins in both the popular and electoral votes.

With the arrival of the new First Family, the social pace in the White House slowed considerably because Mrs. McKinley suffered from epilepsy. Though she insisted on going everywhere with her husband and attending public functions, the excitement of the moment sometimes caused her to faint. When that happened, she did not fall out of her chair, she became rigid. The President, who always sat next to her, would then drape a silk handkerchief over her face until she regained her senses.

No sooner had McKinley taken office than he was confronted with a tense international situation in which Cuba wanted American help to break free of Spanish rule. In spite of pressure from the press, the public and politicians, including his Assistant Secretary of War, Theodore Roosevelt, who called him a "white-livered cur," McKinley refused to commit his country. But when the U.S.S. Maine blew up in Havana harbor on February 15, 1898, the President issued a call for 125,000 volunteers, and the United States declared war on Spain.

Victory in the Spanish-American War, which lasted only 113 days, freed Cuba and gave the United States possession of Guam, the Philippines and Puerto Rico. Congress also annexed Hawaii. Suddenly, this country had thrown off its protective coat of insularity and vaulted into prominence as a world power.

Flushed with the spoils of war and prosperity, the public gave McKinley, his new Vice President, Teddy Roosevelt, the hero of San Juan Hill, and the Republicans a sweeping victory in 1900. The winners' campaign slogan was: "Four more years of the full dinner pail."

McKinley's time was cut short when, six months after his second inaugural, he was mortally wounded by anarchist Leon Czolgosz while attending the Pan American Exposition in Buffalo, New York. The President hung on to life for eight days before succumbing on September 14, 1901, the third Presidential victim of an assassin. His killer was tried, convicted and electrocuted at Auburn State Prison, New York, the following month.

When Theodore Roosevelt succeeded to the Presidency the day McKinley died he was 42 years old, the youngest man to occupy that office. One of his first priorities on moving into the White House with his wife and six children was to get funds from Congress for the total renovation of the century-old building. His efforts coincided with a Congressional decision to do something about the sorry state of the city. Congress had just authorized a special Senate Park Commission, comprised of two architects, a sculptor and a landscape architect, with Senator James McMillan of Michigan as chairman, to develop feasible plans for the future expansion of the city's park system and the government's building program.

Roosevelt gave the responsibility for remodeling the White House, inside and out, to that outstanding architect and president of the American Institute of Architects, Charles McKim, with assistance from Glenn Brown, secretary of the Institute. Then, the Roosevelt family moved to a temporary White House on Lafayette Square. During the next six months, the entire structure was expanded when the two wings that had been built by Thomas Jefferson in 1807 were restored, with the west wing becoming executive offices and the east wing a ceremonial entrance. Internally, workmen installed new plumbing, heating and electrical systems. Rooms were enlarged, including the State Dining Room, staircases moved and rebuilt, ceilings were raised and every room redecorated. To Roosevelt's delight, the mansion was ready in time for the annual New Year's Day reception, 1903.

After considerable research and deliberation, the McMillan Commission concluded that L'Enfant's original design for the city should be resurrected and followed wherever possible. It urged the removal of the railroad station and tracks that turned the Mall into a blighted area, and the building of a Union Station with a large plaza facing the Capitol. The Mall was to be extended to the Potomac, with the filled-in marshland converted into parks. The Commission called for grouping government office buildings in the Federal Triangle, an area between Pennsylvania and Constitution Avenues along the Mall and 15th Street at the base. Since then, 12 buildings have been erected in the Triangle, including those of the Department of Commerce, Department of Labor, Interstate Commerce Commission, Post Office Department, Department of Justice, National Archives and the Bureau of Internal Revenue.

In 1910, Congress created a Commission of Fine Arts and the National Park and Planning Commission to carry out those recommendations.

With the family resettled in the White House, Teddy Roosevelt directed his boundless energies to acquiring the rights to the Panama Canal Zone and starting construction on that waterway. He added the Roosevelt corollary to the Monroe Doctrine by settling a dispute between Venezuela and Germany and Britain, which precluded Germany from attacking Venezuela. He also resolved an Alaskan boundary disagreement between the United States and Britain. Domestically, he led the government's successful attack on the trusts that sought to control the railroads, oil and tobacco. Then, he took time out to get elected in 1904 by the largest majority ever recorded to that time.

In Roosevelt's second term, he helped end the Russo-Japanese War, for which he received the Nobel Peace Prize. Another major event that took almost as much planning and preparation was the incredibly lavish White House wedding of his daughter, dubbed by the press "Princess Alice," to Congressman Nicholas Longworth. Thus began the social reign of Alice Roosevelt Longworth which rivalled that of Dolley Madison in influence and longevity.

Elsewhere in the country, there were definite signs that the United States was on the verge of taking a giant step into the industrial age. First, the Wright brothers made their initial airplane flight at Kitty Hawk, North Carolina. Next, Henry Ford put his first "Model T" on the market.

The Roosevelt years were not all harmony and bliss, however. The city of San Francisco was almost destroyed in 1906 by an earthquake in which almost 500 people died. The following year, the nation was hit by a financial panic brought on by heavy speculation in the stock market.

With the nominating convention of 1908 approaching, Roosevelt threw his support to his Secretary of War, William Howard Taft at the urging of Taft's wife even though he did not really aspire to that office. As a result, Taft was nominated on the first ballot and overwhelmed Democrat William Jennings Bryan at the polls.

The Taft Presidency began on an uncomfortable note . . . and ended on a discordant one. Inauguration Day, March 4, 1909, Washington was gripped by a blizzard so severe that railroad trains could not enter the city, and caused the President-elect to comment, as he took his oath in the Senate Chamber, "Even the elements do protest."

Two months later, Mrs. Taft had a slight stroke that affected her facial muscles. It was at her request that the mayor of Tokyo, the Honorable Yukio Ozaki, presented the city of Washington with 3,000 cherry saplings, which now bloom every spring. Mr. Ozaki got to see the results of his gift when he finally visited Washington in 1950 at the age of 92.

Although the Tafts' social life at the White House never approached the frantic pace of the Roosevelts', they far outdid them when it came to traveling. The Tafts logged 115,000 miles by train over the four-year span. The President also recorded some "firsts" that are interesting. On April 14, 1910, he initiated the Presidential custom of throwing out the first ball of the baseball season. When Arizona was admitted to the Union in 1912, he became the first Chief Executive of the contiguous 48 states. He was still President when the 16th Amendment was ratified authorizing Congress to collect the first taxes on income. Taft later became the first former President to be named Chief Justice of the United States when he was appointed by President Warren G. Harding in 1921. When Taft died in 1930, he was the first President to be interred in the National Cemetery at Arlington.

With election year 1912 getting closer, a political rift developed between Taft and Roosevelt, causing the latter to become the nominee of a splinter group called the Progressive, or "Bull Moose," party. The split divided the Republican vote between Taft and Roosevelt, enabling Democrat Woodrow Wilson to win. Wilson, the Democratic choice on the 46th ballot, was only the second Democrat since the Civil War to be elected. When Taft welcomed his successor to the White House, he said, "I'm glad to be going. This is the lonesomest place in the world."

Great changes took place during the Wilson terms, transforming the essentially simple, provincial country of the 19th century into the modern nation of today. Between the time Wilson was inaugurated on March 4, 1913, until the end of his second term in 1921, Americans learned to be more mobile, putting 8,000,000 cars on the road; skyscrapers rose in large cities; motion pictures became popular entertainment; jazz spread across the country via phonograph records. The 18th Amendment gave the country prohibition, the 19th gave women the right to vote, and the President gave the press the Presidential News Conference.

Life in the White House for Woodrow and Ellen Wilson and their three daughters was relatively quiet. Though the President was essentially a reserved and scholarly man – he had been president of Princeton University – he did have a whimsical strain, and when in a happy mood he might do impersonations, cakewalk or dance a jig. Mrs. Wilson died in August, 1914, after a short illness, and the President married the widow Edith Bolling Galt a year and a half later.

When World War 1 engulfed Europe, Wilson was determined to "be neutral in fact as well as in name." This determination, even in the face of losing American lives aboard the torpedoed British ship, Lusitania, won him re-election in 1916. When the Germans sank several American ships the next year, Wilson went before Congress declaring that "the world must be made safe for democracy." Congress responded by declaring war on Germany on April 6, 1917.

The White House went to war by observing the wheatless and meatless days that Food Administrator Herbert Hoover decreed, and bringing in a flock of sheep to graze on the mansion's lawns. Mrs. Wilson then auctioned off the "White House wool," netting over $100,000 for the Red Cross.

With the successful conclusion of the war, the President and his wife went on a triumphal tour of Europe to sell Europeans on his peace plan, known as the Fourteen Points. Though he had to compromise on some of his points, he did get European agreement to form a League of Nations. Back home, the U.S. Senate refused to ratify the peace treaty, so Wilson, though in a weakened physical condition, undertook a cross-country speaking tour to sell the American public on the League. He collapsed in Kansas, returned to the White House and suffered a paralytic stroke on October 3, 1919. He was invalided for the rest of his life, but he did not give up his office. He left his bed only for simple recreation or for purely formal tasks like signing official documents.

The League failed to win Senate approval, and when it became a plank in the Democratic platform in 1920, it helped the Republican nominee, Warren G. Harding, defeat the ticket of James M. Cox and Franklin Delano Roosevelt. One month later, Woodrow Wilson was awarded the Nobel Peace Prize for his work in seeking a fair peace agreement and founding the League of Nations. On his death in 1924, Wilson was interred in the National Cathedral, thereby becoming the only President buried in Washington, D.C.

Tired of wartime restraints and world problems, and wanting to turn back the clock to regain the more carefree pre-war way of life, American voters found Harding's campaign slogan, "Back to Normalcy," very appealing. For a short time after the inauguration, it appeared as though the voters would get their wish. The White House quickly became the focal point of a brilliant social season that included all the official state receptions and dinners that had been discontinued because of the war and then Wilson's poor health. During that time, the Lincoln Memorial was finished and dedicated. But soon thereafter, Harding's administration was buffeted first by a severe depression and then by the beginning of what would become a succession of scandals involving the "Ohio gang," friends the President had put in high places.

In an attempt to revive public confidence, Harding embarked on a cross-country speaking tour with his wife that included the first Presidential visit to Canada and Alaska. Harding became ill on the West Coast and died in San Francisco on August 2, 1923, the sixth President to die in office. The exact cause of his death was never determined.

Vice President Calvin Coolidge was vacationing on the family's Vermont farm when he was notified of Harding's death. His father, Colonel John Calvin Coolidge, a notary public and Justice of the Peace, administered the oath of office in the early hours of the morning by the light of a kerosene lamp in the sitting room. This marked the only time a President had been sworn in by his father!

Coolidge finished out that Presidential term and then won election on his own. Though his wife, Grace, was known for her cheerful, outgoing disposition, "Silent Cal," a thrifty, laconic New Englander, seemed totally out of step with the exuberant mood of the Roaring 20's. He rarely smiled, even on happy occasions such as entertaining Charles Lindbergh, just back from his solo flight across the Atlantic. At one such affair, a lady bet him that she could get more than two words out of him. Answered the President: "You lose." His most famous statement, however, was made while on summer vacation in the Black Hills of South Dakota in 1927. He called newsmen to his office in the Rapid City high school and handed each one a slip of paper that read: "I do not choose to run for President in 1928."

Before leaving the White House, the Coolidges improved the living quarters by adding rooms at the top level and a sunroom above the south portico.

As soon as Coolidge declared himself out of the race, the Republicans unhesitatingly opted for Herbert Hoover on the first ballot. Their decision was upheld by the voters who made Hoover their clear choice over Democrat Alfred E. Smith.

No two couples could be more patently different than the Hoovers and the Coolidges. The Hoovers were cosmopolitan, very wealthy, philanthropic and lavish spenders. It has been said that the President even turned his salary back to the U.S. Treasury. The Hoovers reportedly enjoyed the best table ever set in the White House up until then, which met with instant approval from Washington society.

The prosperity of the Roaring 20's came to a crashing halt when the stock market plunged on October 29, 1929, just eight months after Hoover's inauguration, marking the start of the Great Depression. Despite his genius for organization and his unswerving faith in his dream for America of "two chickens in every pot and a car in every garage," he could not stop the downward slide of the economy or the relentless rise of unemployment. As thousands of people lost their homes, many were reduced to living in clusters of shacks that became known as "Hoovervilles."

When 15,000 World War I veterans marched on Washington asking that their promised bonuses be paid immediately, the House voted for payment but the Senate voted against it. Hoover sided with the Senate and ordered U.S. Army troops, under the command of General Douglas MacArthur, to drive the veterans out of the city.

Amid increasing unemployment figures as well as bank and business failures, Hoover was decisively defeated in 1932 by Democrat Franklin Delano Roosevelt, who promised the people a "New Deal."

Not since the Teddy Roosevelt Presidency had the White House been the focus of such excitement and anticipation as the Franklin Delano Roosevelts brought to it in March, 1933. FDR, as he was soon to be known, had swept to victory to the tune of "Happy Days Are Here Again" and he intended to make that a reality. "The only thing we have to fear," he told the American people in his inaugural address, "is fear itself." With that, he called Congress into a special session, and for the next hundred days, he submitted recovery and reform laws, and Congress passed them, mostly by large majorities. The country got another kind of lift when the 21st Amendment was ratified, repealing prohibition.

Meanwhile, Eleanor Roosevelt spent time adapting the White House to the needs of her family when she was not traveling around the country, serving as "eyes and ears" for her husband. An indoor swimming pool was installed so FDR could exercise his polio-crippled legs. Then, the executive offices in the west wing were enlarged and a new Cabinet Room added. A third-floor tier of offices were created, and the east wing was also enlarged. The White House kitchen was made electric, and for the first time, an electric dishwasher was put in. Some years later, when the United States was at war, the east wing was remodeled to accommodate Secret Service agents, and a subterranean bomb shelter was built in the basement. During World War II, FDR used the White House as a symbol of America's unity with its war-ravaged allies by refusing to have the exterior painted, no matter how shabby-looking it became.

As FDR strove to put America back to work and give the economy a lift through the New Deal, he won re-election in 1936 by a bigger majority than previously, collecting the electoral votes of every state except the eight from Maine and Vermont. The country was slowly emerging from the Great Depression when a greater calamity struck Europe. Germany invaded Poland on September 1, 1939, and World War II had begun. FDR did what he could to aid the Allies, without committing American soldiers, by arranging to send them material and equipment through Lend-Lease agreements. These conditions lasted until December 7, 1941, when the Japanese bombed Pearl Harbor. By this time, FDR was into an unprecedented third term, and the United States was now into the war.

Entertaining at the White House was curtailed as FDR became completely immersed in the conduct of the war and meeting with allied leaders in various parts of the world to agree on the grand strategy. But then, not long after his fourth inauguration, and soon after a meeting with Churchill and Stalin at Yalta, FDR died at the Little White House in Warm Springs, Georgia. The date was April 12, 1945.

After 12 years in the White House, few people knew more about the taxing demands of the Presidency than Eleanor Roosevelt. She met her husband's successor in her study to tell him: "Harry, the President is dead." And when Vice President Truman asked, "Is there anything I can do for you?" Mrs. Roosevelt solicitously replied: "Is there anything we can do for you? For you are the one in trouble now."

When he talked with newsmen the next day, the 33rd President said: "Boys, if you ever pray, pray for me now." Despite his own misgivings, and to the chagrin of his detractors, Harry S. Truman, the outspoken, piano-playing former haberdasher, proved to be more than capable of meeting his new responsibilities. Within a month after his inauguration, Germany surrendered and Truman proclaimed May 8, his 61st birthday, as V-E Day (Victory in Europe Day). Then, in rapid succession, the United Nations Charter was signed by 50 nations in San Francisco in June (it was ratified in October). Truman met with Churchill and Stalin at Potsdam in July to agree on peace terms for Germany. The following month saw the beginning of the Atomic Age when Truman ordered the bombing of Hiroshima and Nagasaki, bringing the war with Japan to an end (V-J Day).

Other Truman first-term accomplishments were: (a) the Truman Doctrine, guaranteeing American aid to any free nation resisting communist aggression; (b) the Marshall Plan, offering economic assistance to war-damaged nations in Europe; (c) the Berlin Airlift that broke the Russian blockade to Berlin by supplying the city with food and coal. Truman did not fare nearly as well on the home front when he tried to continue Roosevelt's "New Deal" policies with his own "Fair Deal" and ran into Congressional opposition that included members of his own party. When he decided to run in 1948, Truman was nominated on the first ballot, causing two dissident groups to bolt the convention. The Liberal group then formed the Progressive party and nominated one-time Vice President Henry Wallace. The other group, Southern Democrats who opposed Truman's civil rights program, organized the Dixiecrat party and nominated South Carolina's Governor, J. Strom Thurmond.

With the Democratic vote split three ways, the Republican candidate, Thomas E. Dewey, was virtually conceded the election by everyone except one man, Harry Truman. Embarking on a whistle-stop campaign by train, he traveled 31,000 miles, made more than 350 speeches and achieved the biggest political upset in American history.

Instead of returning to the White House, however, the Truman family moved across Pennsylvania Avenue to Blair House, where they lived until March, 1952. The reason: the White House had become so weak structurally that only total renovation and rebuilding could save it from falling down. As the Commissioner of Public Buildings remarked: "The second floor was staying up there purely from habit." It took three years and approximately $5,500,000 to do the job, including the addition of a balcony over the south portico that the President wanted.

Once again, Truman's term was filled with far-reaching, difficult decisions. The United States signed the North Atlantic Pact, creating NATO and committing to defend Western Europe against Soviet aggression. Next, Communist soldiers from North Korea invaded South Korea, and Truman sent American troops, under General Douglas MacArthur, in the vanguard of United Nations forces. The President later removed MacArthur, despite a great public furor, when he found his authority challenged. By the time election year 1952 came around, Truman had had enough and declined to run, saying, "I have served my country long, and I think efficiently and honestly. I do not feel that it is my duty to spend another four years in the White House."

Persuaded by the Republicans to run in 1952, after rejecting two previous overtures, Dwight David Eisenhower, former

Supreme Commander of Allied Forces in Europe, showed that he still had the complete trust of the American people. His campaign to "clean up the mess in Washington," and his promise to go to Korea to help end the war, led the Republicans to a clean sweep of the White House and both Houses of Congress. True to his pledge, Eisenhower flew to Korea shortly after the election. The war ended in July, 1953.

During Eisenhower's first term, the country was shaken by an inquisition-like investigation of alleged Communists in the government by a Senate subcommittee. The investigation died when it proved to have little substance to sustain it, and the Senate censured the committee chairman, Joseph McCarthy, a junior colleague from Wisconsin. The term McCarthyism has since become a synonym for witch-hunting. Another issue of much greater concern was the Supreme Court's landmark decision in the case of Brown vs. the Board of Education of Topeka, outlawing racial segregation in public schools. This decision met with considerable resistance, particularly in the South, and caused the President to send U.S. troops to Little Rock, Arkansas, to protect black students trying to enroll in white schools.

There was some question about Eisenhower running for a second term in 1956, because he had suffered a heart attack and undergone an emergency operation for ileitis. But he regained his health and his lease on the White House while the voters chanted "We like Ike." They may have liked the man but they did not like the party, because the Republicans lost control of Congress.

An avid golfer, Ike became a familiar sight to passers-by who could see him practicing his golf shots on a special green that was installed for him on the White House lawn. He also enjoyed cooking and frequently invited close friends to a cookout on the White House roof, where he took over the job of broiling the steaks on a charcoal grill.

On October 4, 1957, the world was suddenly lifted into the Space Age when Russia launched Sputnik I, the first man-made satellite, followed by Sputnik II one month later. The United States entered its own vehicle in the race when it fired Explorer I into space on January 31, 1958. The National Aeronautics and Space Administration (NASA) was established six months later.

Two entries of a different kind occurred in 1959 when Alaska and Hawaii were admitted to statehood, making Eisenhower the first President of all 50 states. And as the country expanded, so did the Capitol. On July 4, the President laid the cornerstone for an extension of the Capitol's east front that would add two and a half acres of floor space, the first major expansion of the historic building in almost a century.

With his second term coming to an end (the 22nd

Amendment now restricted Presidents to two full elected terms), Ike found his prestige abroad slipping. The Russians cancelled a summit meeting after shooting down a U.S. spy plane, and Fidel Castro brought on a diplomatic break by seizing all American-owned property in Cuba. Thus, it was with few regrets that the old soldier looked forward to retirement on his recently-purchased Gettysburg farm, his permanent home since entering West Point. The Republican banner was passed on to his Vice President of the past eight years, Richard M. Nixon.

Opposing Nixon in the 1960 election was Democrat John F. Kennedy, a young Massachusetts Senator and World War II combat hero. The election turned on a series of four television debates, which showed Kennedy off to better advantage than his Republican opponent. By fewer than 120,000 popular votes, but 303 to 219 electoral votes, Kennedy became the youngest (43) elected President and the first Roman Catholic to take over the White House.

Washington welcomed Jack Kennedy, his stylishly elegant young wife, Jacqueline, and two small children, plus a prolific and energetic Kennedy clan. Jackie took over the redecoration of the White House as her favorite project and made the old mansion into a historic showplace. She also became a trend setter for clothing and hair styles and drew crowds of admirers wherever she went. Her popularity reached the point where at a Paris luncheon honoring the Kennedys the President laughingly began his speech: "I am the man who accompanied Jacqueline Kennedy . . ."

Making good on his campaign promise to lead Americans to a "New Frontier," JFK launched the Peace Corps to help people in developing nations raise their standards of living. He fought for equal rights for blacks at home, using U.S. marshals and federal troops when necessary to enforce desegregation of Southern colleges and public schools. He requested sweeping civil rights legislation from Congress, declaring, "The time has come for the Congress of the United States to join with the executive and judicial branches in making clear to all that race has no place in American life or law."

On another frontier, Alan B. Shepard, Jr., was the first American to make a suborbital flight. It lasted 15 minutes. Then, ten months later, John H. Glenn, Jr., became the first American to orbit the earth.

In foreign affairs, the President suffered an embarrassing setback when Cuban rebels staged an unsuccessful assault landing at the Bay of Pigs in an attempt to overthrow Fidel Castro's Communist government. JFK accepted the blame for that disaster. When the Russians tried to arm Cuba with long-range missiles, Kennedy ordered a naval blockade of Cuba until the missiles were removed. But in Europe, the Russians set up their own blockade when they built the wall that now separates East and West Berlin.

On November 22, 1963, the world was stunned by the news that President Kennedy had been shot as he rode through the streets of Dallas, Texas. He died at 1:00 p.m. in a local hospital without regaining consciousness. At 2:39 p.m., a U.S. District Judge administered the oath of office to Vice President Lyndon Baines Johnson aboard the Presidential airplane. The President's assassin, Lee Harvey Oswald, was himself shot to death 48 hours later by Jack Ruby, a Dallas nightclub owner. Representatives from over 90 countries attended John F. Kennedy's funeral on November 25. He was interred at Arlington Cemetery, the second President to be buried there and the fourth one to die from an assassin's bullet.

Lyndon B. Johnson, 36th President of the United States, had originally been a candidate for the Presidential nomination at the Democratic convention in 1960. But when Jack Kennedy was chosen on the first ballot, he offered the second spot to Johnson, who accepted it. By a strange twist of fate, Lyndon Johnson was the first Southerner (Texas) to become President since another Johnson (Andrew) succeeded to the office after the assassination of Lincoln almost 100 years earlier.

A veteran of 24 years in Congress, Johnson needed all his expertise and experience to manage the problems he inherited. He told Congress that: "This nation will keep its commitments from South Vietnam to West Berlin." That meant continuing to lend U.S. technical and financial support to South Vietnam which was under attack by Communist-supported Viet Cong guerrillas from North Vietnam. When North Vietnam torpedo boats attacked American destroyers in the Gulf of Tonkin, the President ordered U.S. Navy planes to bomb their bases.

At home, Johnson proposed a "War on Poverty" to create new jobs and build up areas that needed economic assistance. He persuaded Congress to cut individual and corporate taxes. And he signed a civil rights bill that opened to blacks all hotels, motels, restaurants, and any businesses serving the public. It also guaranteed equal job opportunities for all.

In 1964, Johnson and his running mate, Hubert H. Humphrey, scored a landslide victory over Republicans Barry M. Goldwater and William E. Miller by holding out the hope of a "Great Society." If the Congress would adopt his domestic programs, LBJ had said, ". . . we have the opportunity to move not only toward the rich society, but upward to the Great Society."

But, 1965 saw the fighting in Vietnam spread, and the U.S. military effort begin to escalate beyond the original intention. Domestically, large Democratic majorities in Congress enabled Johnson to get many of his proposals passed such as aid to education, Medicare for the elderly and economic help for an 11-state Appalachian Mountains region. The President also came to the aid of Washington, D.C. by reorganizing the District's government to give residents the greatest measure of self-government since Congress took control in 1874. The 23rd Amendment, ratified in 1961, gave D.C. residents the right to vote in national elections. Now, Johnson set up the post of commissioner, plus a nine-member city council, all appointed by the President, whose make-up would reflect the city's predominantly black population and would represent the city in dealing with Congress. This was one step closer to home rule.

When it came time for the 1968 nominating conventions, LBJ was eligible for one more term but he declined to run. The U.S. involvement in Vietnam had deeply divided the country, and, in addition, the President had lost Congressional support for his Great Society programs.

Although some people had written him off politically after he lost the Presidential election in 1960 and the 1962 race for the governorship of California, Richard Milhous Nixon was a man of dogged determination. He made a triumphant return by winning the Republican Presidential nomination in 1968 on the first ballot, and then beat the Democratic candidate and incumbent Vice President, Hubert H. Humphrey, for the highest office. But what started with such a resurgence of faith and optimism later turned into condemnation and disgrace.

Then, in the election year of 1972, the first cracks began to show in the Nixon administration's credibility. On June 17, seven men were arrested for illegally breaking and entering Democratic National Committee headquarters at the Watergate complex with the intent to plant bugging equipment. Though the men were tied to the Committee to Re-elect the President, the incident appeared to be minor and was investigated by the FBI.

Nixon was renominated and re-elected with 96.6 percent of the electoral votes to Democrat George McGovern's 3.4 percent. Vietnam peace talks were resumed, and in January, 1973, a cease-fire agreement was signed in Paris by the United States, North and South Vietnam and the Viet Cong provisional government.

The Watergate investigation, however, began to take on much larger dimensions as more and more White House staffers were implicated. Then, the Senate set up the Select Committee to Investigate Watergate, chaired by Sam J. Ervin of North Carolina, and when that group unearthed proof of a cover-up, the Attorney General and the two chief White House aides resigned, and the President's counsel was dismissed. Further investigation by special Watergate prosecutor Archibald Cox revealed the existence of tapes that indicated many of Nixon's close associates had a role in the cover-up, including, allegedly, the President himself. When Cox tried to subpoena the tapes, Nixon fired him. Later, a new prosecutor, Leon Jaworski, was named.

As the web of evidence tightened around the Presidency, including some unexplained gaps in certain critical tapes that had been turned over to the U.S. District Court, the public and Congressional clamor for either Nixon's resignation or impeachment reached the point where he could no longer "tough it out." On August 9, 1974, Richard M. Nixon became the first President to resign, leaving the capital immediately for his home in San Clemente, California, without waiting to see Gerald Ford sworn in as the 38th President.

There can be little doubt that the Founding Fathers never conceived of anyone attaining the Presidency the way Gerald R. Ford did it. As the first President to hold the nation's two top posts without being elected to either, he was acutely aware of the awkwardness of his position. In his brief inaugural statement, he appealed to the American people for their understanding and aid: ". . . you have not elected me as your President by your ballots. So I ask you to confirm me as your President with your prayers . . . I have not campaigned either for the Presidency or the Vice Presidency. I have not subscribed to any partisan platform. I am indebted to no man, and only to one woman – my dear wife – as I begin the most difficult job in the world. I have not sought this tremendous responsibility, but I will not shirk it . . ."

Thus, the man, actually born Leslie Lynch King, Jr., but who changed his name when adopted by his stepfather, Gerald Rudolf Ford, tried to bring normalcy back to the White House. Unfortunately, his decision to grant his predecessor "a full, free and absolute pardon" brought an angry outraged response from the public, though it was too late to change it because the President's pardon is irrevocable. Next, he alienated many conservative Republicans by choosing liberal-leaning Nelson A. Rockefeller as his Vice President.

During his two and a half years in office, Ford had the FBI and CIA reorganized after a special Rockefeller Commission discovered they were involved in the Watergate cover up, as well as many illegal and unauthorized activities at home and abroad. He vetoed 66 bills, survived two assassination attempts by women (Lynette Alice Fromme and Sara Jane Moore) who are now serving life sentences, and signed the White House Bicentennial Independence proclamation calling for the simultaneous ringing of bells throughout the country on July 4, 1976, for two minutes at 2 p.m. Eastern Standard Time.

Washington's residents had an additional reason to celebrate. They now had a charter, approved by Congress, that moved them another step closer to self-determination. Under the new charter, they elected a mayor, a 13-member

City Council and a network of neighborhood councils to advise the central council on such local issues as planning, sanitation, zoning and recreation. The new government had the power to tax but Congress retained the right of ultimate judgment on spending proposals. As one resident described the arrangement: "It is a partnership, with Congress being the major partner."

Ford decided he wanted to run in 1976, and the Republicans nominated him despite some strong opposition from the Governor of California, Ronald Reagan. But Ford's caretaker Presidency came to an end when the Democratic candidate from Plains, Georgia, James Earl Carter, Jr. ("My name is Jimmy Carter and I'm running for President"), squeaked in by a margin of only two percent of the popular vote, but a 297 to 240 advantage in electoral votes.

The Carter administration was marked by a reduction in pomp and ceremony – he walked up Pennsylvania Avenue with his wife after the inauguration, and requested that "Hail to the Chief" not be played whenever he put in an official appearance. Entertaining at the White House was also put on a simpler, less formal basis.

Jimmy Carter scored a notable success in the eyes of the world when he brought the leaders of Egypt and Israel together at Camp David, where they reached agreement for a formal peace treaty. He caused considerable consternation in the United States, however, when he signed two treaties with Panama, one turning the canal over to Panama in 1999, and the other committing the United States to defend it from 1999 on. Not many people knew that negotiations on both points had been going on since 1964.

The one incident that shocked the American people, and doomed Carter's hope for re-election, occurred on November 4, 1979, when the U.S. embassy in Teheran was stormed by Iranian rebel students and 66 Americans were made captives. This began a 14-month ordeal for the captives and for American authorities trying to negotiate their release with the various and sometimes conflicting political segments in control. After months of fruitless negotiations and one abortive rescue attempt, agreement was reached. The hostages were released on January 20, 1981, minutes after Ronald Reagan had been sworn in as the 40th President of the United States.

Thinking he could repeat his victory of '76, Carter had decided to run again. He received the nomination on the first ballot, but public confidence in his administration had been so eroded that Republican Reagan was never really challenged. He won by more than 8,500,000 popular votes and 90 percent of the electoral votes.

Ronald Reagan was the oldest President to be inaugurated (69 years and 349 days), and the first one to have been a professional actor. With the arrival of Ronald and Nancy (she had been a professional actress) Reagan, Washington society looked forward to a revival of more glamorous White House happenings. Although Reagan was elected as a political conservative who promised to cut government spending and taxes, his inauguration reportedly cost $8,000,000 and was said to be the most expensive one in American history.

On March 30, 1981, as he left the Washington Hilton Hotel after addressing a group of union officials, President Reagan was shot in the chest. His assailant also wounded the President's press secretary, a Secret Service agent and a policeman. All the victims, though severely wounded, survived. The assailant was captured, tried, found innocent by reason of insanity and committed to a mental institution.

The United States entered the decade of the 80's with rampant inflation, soaring interest rates, sagging production and declining morale. But while the rest of the country was suffering through a mental and economic depression, the city of Washington became the boom town that the original builders and landowners had hoped for when the city was first planned. Buildings began going up all over the downtown area to accommodate the influx of corporate representatives, lobbyists, trade associations, high tech companies, brokerage firms and legal advisers.

Statistically, Washington is now the nation's 15th largest city, with a population larger than that of four states. Only 21 percent of the area's population lives in the District of Columbia, the rest spilling over into four counties of Virginia and three in Maryland. As of April, 1980, more than 3,000,000 people resided in this, the country's eighth largest metropolitan area, ranking just behind San Francisco and slightly ahead of Dallas-Fort Worth.

Even though it has a sizable poor black population clustered in the District and Prince Georges County, Maryland, the median family income for Washington is $27,515, compared with $19,908 nationally.

Washington has also taken on the cultural accoutrements and sophistication of a major city, with its own opera, symphony, ballet and legitimate theater. It has a proliferation of new restaurants to fit every pocketbook and ethnic taste, branches of the country's major department stores and numerous new art galleries and museums. It has finally thrown off the sleepy Southern antebellum image and become more like the imperial city imagined by Pierre L'Enfant when he stood atop Jenkins' Hill and envisioned his dream city rising out of the forests and marshlands. Wonder what he would say if he could see it now.

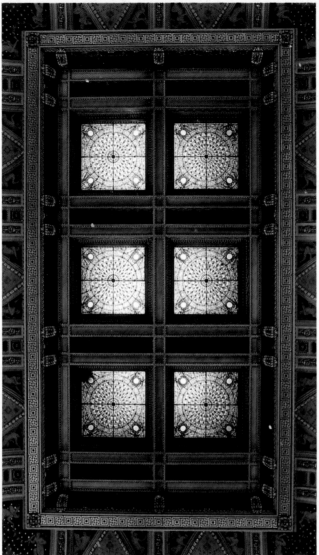

Constructed at the turn of the century, the Library of Congress Building *these pages* houses one of the largest and finest collections of books in the world, including such priceless treasures as the Gutenberg Bible. As well as serving its many visiting readers, the library also provides Congress with an invaluable research service. Full of fascinating architectural embellishment, the library complex has grown considerably since its opening in 1897.

The marble staircase *above* **leads to the superb circular Main Reading Room with its fine dome and lantern. The imposing Great Hall** *facing page* **of the Library of Congress, its vaulted ceiling supported by a mass of pillars and arches, is typical of the Italian Renaissance style of the building.**

The quiet, tree-lined streets of suburban Washington with their tidy town houses and apartment buildings *this page* are little different from those in the residential areas of any other major city. *Facing page:* a barge laboriously negotiates a series of locks in the Chesapeake and Ohio canal which runs through the Georgetown area of the city.

Wisconsin Avenue and M Street are two of the main shopping thoroughfares in the popular and often exclusive Georgetown district. Here fine cooking can be enjoyed in one of the many varied restaurants *right and top right*, a few lazy hours can be spent gazing into the attractive shop windows, admiring the floral displays *far right center and bottom* or relaxing over a cup of coffee in the flower-scented atmosphere above the Georgetown Park Florist *facing page*. Washington nightlife *top* is as vibrant and varied as that of any other city, with no shortage of pubs, clubs and discotheques.

Viewed from the top of the 555-foot high Washington
Monument, the Mall sweeps gracefully towards the
Capitol Building at its eastern end *above*. Lined by such
famous institutions as the Smithsonian, the National
Gallery of Art and the Museum of Natural History, the
Mall is flanked by Constitution and Independence
Avenues to the left and right in the picture. *Facing page:*
the White House and its grounds, with 16th Street beyond.

The city of Washington *above,* stands on the flat, undis-
tinguished land of the Atlantic Coastal Plain – an area
originally composed of swampy lowland whose highest
point is only some 400 feet above sea level. Carefully
developed since its original foundation, the city has grown
to become one of the most spectacular of the world's
capitals. *Facing page:* bound for Washington's Dulles
International Airport, a plane descends over the misty,
tree-lined banks of the Potomac River.

The Mall *left* gives the sightseer a superb, uninterrupted view of the Capitol Building's symmetrical beauty. With the aptly named Reflecting Pool in front and the Potomac River behind, the classic shape of the Lincoln Memorial *above* honors one of the nation's greatest leaders. Home of all American Presidents except George Washington, the White House *facing page* is probably the most famous of all Washington buildings.

Carved in the black granite walls of the Vietnam Veterans Memorial in the Mall are the names of the 57,939 Americans who made the ultimate sacrifice for their country. The memorial *these pages,* paid for by private donations and designed by Maya Ying Lin, draws large crowds; relatives, comrades and fellow Americans, who come to honor the courage and devotion to duty of those who lost their lives in Vietnam.

THOMAS E HARTUNG • RAYMOND H HEYRICK
KEENER • ROBERT D MERRELL • GEORGE A MORGAN •
RDUE • ALLEN L PIERCE • DONALD C PIPER • WILLIE PIPPINS Sr •
TFIELD BENNIE LEE SIMMONS • FREDERICK A SLEMP • CECIL Y WARE •
TOMMIE LEE WILLIAMS • JESSE J BOLTON • FRANKLIN V BRODNIK •
CHOLES SOCHACKI • JAMES M TERMINI • CLYDE W WITHEE •
ALLEY • SIMMIE BELLAMY Jr • ELMER E BERRY • THOMAS C BREWER Jr •
EE IRVIN CLARKE Jr • CHARLIES E DANIELS • JOHNSON F FRANK •
AM JACK L HIMES • ROBERT L HOSKINS Jr • DANIEL R JAMES •
TCHELL • DONALD S NEWTON • ROBERT D WILLIAMS Jr • FREDERICK E SMITH •
RY • BILLIE N PLUM • FRANCIS D WILLS • WILLIAM F AYRES •
GRAVES • PAUL E HELSEL Jr • RICK E KOPKA • LAWRENCE B McCLOUD •
TH • JAMES M SPENCE • ROGER D BULIFANT • HENRY C CASEBOLT •
R H CLEGG • PETER W FIELDS • WILLIAM FUCHS Jr • FRANKLIN D R GILBERT •
BISZ • ARTHUR J JACKSON • MARSHALL JESSIE • CHARLES JOHNSON •
ES B LAIRD • RAYMOND E MEYERS • KENNETH D MIDDLETON • MARK L MORGAN •
RD J McCARTHY • BRENT A McCLELLAN • GEORGE F McCOY • CURTIS J McGEE •
McGUIRE Jr • JAMES R McLEMORE • JOSE TORRES • RICHARD J WOLCHESKI •
C PEDERSON • MICHAEL D PLISKA • DARRELL T RAY • ALBERT C ROBERTS •
ROGERS • CHARLES W SIMS • CLIFTON L TART • MIGUEL E NARANJO Jr •
AM M CHRISTENSEN • WILLIAM P FORAN • CHARLIE M YOUNG • ALBERT F BAIRD •
DS R HATCHER • MARSHALL M HOLT Jr • DONALD J WOLOS... • RONNIE R KING •
WORST • CHARLES F COINER • JACK M HO... • DONALD...
NIS OGLESBY III • CHARLES W RADER • ROBERT F FIELDER... • ...NETT... BOBLISH •
EPHEN P ALSTED • STUART M ANDREWS • DENNIS L TA...GTON • ...GREENE •
BAKER III • DANIEL P BIRCH • RAYMOND BLANCHETTE • HERIBERTO ARMENTA • GARY C ALLEN •
MES E BUSH • RUPERT S CARVEN III • PHILLIP H CLARK • JAMES S COCCHIARA •
RICHARD P CORSON • BRUCE DAVIS • STANLEY T DEMBOSKI • WILLIAM W BROWN •
REUBEN L GARNETT Jr • ANDREW L HASTINGS • SEAN P DODSON • LESTER R ATHERDEN •
DAVID M HANN • JOHN M HARDEN • RONALD W GODDARD • HARRY M GODWIN •
S HERRON • JOHNNY RAY HOLLOWAY • MICHAEL A GILSON • HARRY P HELT Jr •
NZ J KOLBECK • HARVEY W JONES • HENRY J HOOPER • WILLIAM J HRINKO •
NALD R LUMLEY • ROBERT B LABBE • ARNELL KEYES • LEWIS A KIMMEL Jr •
SAMUEL G ORLANDO • DIEGO MERCADO • JACK W LINDSEY • FRANK LOPEZ •
DONNELL D McMILLIN • PAUL G PARSONS • VINFORD F MICHAEL • PETER G SCAVUZZO •
ROBERT B... • DELBERT L TRUBE Jr • JAMES R SCOTT • JACKIE D REYNOLDS • JOSEPH R REYNOLDS •
LES V... • LEWIS D BELL • LESTER A WESICHAN • ROSCOE L VICK • ALFRED J SMITH •
OWN ALBERT CABANACAN • MICHAEL MAX BARNWELL • CHARLES R WETZEL • CHARLES D WADSWORTH •
I DOSTER • JAMES H BIANCHINI • DAVID L BAUMGARDNER • MICHAEL R YOUNG •
WILLIAM R EMMONS • ROBERT MALLENDA CALIBOSO • KENNETH A BRADLEY • WILLIE JOE BRAMLET •
NOS GONZALES Jr • JOSEPH C EVANS Jr • PHILIP FITCH • ROBERT C HESSOM •
DARRELL JOHNSON • ROY H HARBISON • STEVEN A CHURCH • THOMAS W EDWARDS •
UNFORD DENNIS H LYDEN • LEONARD A HULTQUIST • RICKEY D GARNER •
WILLIAM McCLURE • JOSE E LACUE • LOUIS J HERNANDEZ • THOMAS A JENNINGS • CHARLES E CRUTCHFIELD •
SAMUEL RODRIGUEZ • PAUL I MAHER • MARIO C KITTS • FREDERICK G LYNCH •
ROBERTO McSWAIN • ... SHIELDS • DANNY A NETH • TOMMY R MILLER •
GALEN... JOHN...

JAMES L TEWKSBURY • CURTIS E D...
DAVID M DAVIES • DONALD R BUR...
WILLIAM D HASTY • JAMES MOOR...
NORMAN N MILLER • PAUL R HATTA...
THURMAN W OWEN • DANIEL J PIC...
KEITH L SHIPP • JIMMY B TAYLOR • LE...
RALPH M WILLIAMS • RICHARD H W...
GARY D NAIL • DAVID E HORNBY • R...
ARTHUR C MORRIS Jr • KENNETH D C...
DONOVAN J PRUETT • TOMMIE LEE S...
JACK D GILBERT • FRANKLIN E HOSLE...
JAMES W BROWN • GERMAN CHAPAR...
KEITH W KAUFFMAN • HAROLD W LO...
LAWRENCE McCREA • CHARLIE REED ...
EDWARD M STANCHEK • FRANKLIN F W...
ARNOLD WOODSON • BERNARD BAR...
DENNIS P COOK • JAMES W GATES • JA...
ROBERT A KREUZIGER • JOHN W LAFAYE...
THOMAS J RALSTON • JACK A SMITH • R...
JOHN M BROWN III • MARTIN COX • WA...
ARTHUR J BAYLOR • THOMAS T WALKER •
GEORGE L SAMUELS • CHARLES M SHEL...
RALPH S KOROLZYK • THOMAS W MUIR ...
RONALD T SHELTON • TOM K TINGLE • LO...
HOWARD C BLEVINS • RICHARD F BUBAL...
RALPH COLEMAN • ZED C CREVELING • JO...
JOHN H EAGLIN • PHILYAW FEE • JO...
DONALD W HALL • DAVID A HAMMETT • EL...
PHILIP A JONES • EVERETT E LANGSTON •
RICHARD NOYOLA • JAMES W ROBINSON ...
EDWARD W REILLY • CHARLES D OGLESBY •
J C LESLIE SHORT • JOSEPH F SMITH • THOMA...
GEORGE H WARD • JOHN W WATKINS •
LAVALL DURR • WILLIAM A GLASSON • ERIC...
EDMUND H HORNSTEIN • RONNIE RAY LOVE...
COLEY L WASHINGTON • FRED A BENNER •
JESSE L CLARK II • GREEN CONLEY • FRANK A D...
LLOYD FIELDS Jr • PHILLIPS LAMARR • FRANK A D...
JOSE A PACHECO • RONALD G SOULE • RICHARD...
JOHN C MAPE • JIMMY RAY WOLFE • JAMES...
CHARLES J MURPHY Jr • BURTON K McCO...
LEWIS M THOMAS • ROBERT...
RALPH H LIVESAY • DENNIS...
WALTER H ... • JOHN...

The leaf-strewn walkways that border the Mall *above* are a popular haunt of joggers and cyclists as well as sightseers who can take in the elegance of the surrounding buildings. From the Capitol end of Madison Drive *right* can be seen the dark outlines of the Smithsonian Institution while *far right* is the distinctive, circular shape of the neighboring Hirshhorn Museum. *Facing page:* the monolithic Washington Monument soars above the trees at the Mall's western end.

Tracing the relatively recent history of man's airborne achievements, the twenty-four galleries of the National Air and Space Museum *these pages,* part of the enormous Smithsonian Institution, house a unique collection of fascinating exhibits. The craft on display range from some of the earliest and most primitive machines, as used by the pioneers of flight, to the ultra-sophisticated rockets, missiles and lunar modules of the space-age era. The static displays are supported by many interesting slide and film shows that make a visit to this most popular of museums an exciting and unforgettable experience.

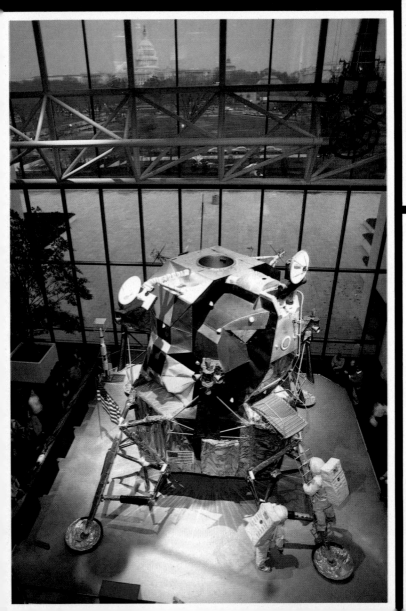

Washington's Episcopal Church of St. Peter and St. Paul, widely known as the Washington National Cathedral, stands on Mount St. Albans on the northwest outskirts of the city. Adorning the sanctuary *facing page* is the magnificent stone screen, its central panel dominated by the figure of "Christ in Majesty." The Cathedral's many stained-glass windows, their scenes depicted in the modern idiom *bottom left,* are particularly striking, as are the superb wood-carvings in the delightful Children's Chapel *below and bottom right.*

Occupying some 500 acres on the sloping, peaceful shores of the Potomac River is the Arlington National Cemetery. Once a part of the District of Columbia, Arlington County was returned to the state of Virginia and the cemetery stands on land that was owned by Robert E. Lee. Laid to rest in this famous burial ground that traces its origins back to the Civil War are such famous names as John F. Kennedy *far right*, William Howard Taft and General John Pershing, although far more numerous are the modest headstones bearing names of ordinary soldiers killed in action *above, right and facing page*. The Memorial Amphitheatre *top right*, which adjoins the Tomb of the Unknown Soldier, is used for Memorial and Veteran Day services.

The enormous African elephant in the building's Rotunda *above* and the awe-inspiring skeletal remains in the Hall of Dinosaurs *facing page* are just a few of the breathtaking exhibits that can be viewed in Washington's Museum of Natural History. The museum's diverse collection of more than 60 million items cover the development of the world since the time of the Ice Age.

Washington's many fine art galleries such as the National, Corcoran and Freer, contain a superb selection of works of art representing most of the world's major schools and movements. Always popular with the many visitors are the paintings by great American artists such as Copley *left. Bottom left:* the Explorer's Hall, with its enormous globe, in the National Geographic Society Building. *Facing page:* the city's modern Metro system, with its quiet, comfortable trains and helpful attendants, is the ideal way to get around the town quickly.

Softly mirrored in the glass-like surface of the Reflecting Pool, the gold-lit Washington Monument stands out against a purple night sky *above. Facing page:* **from its eternal seat in the magnificent memorial building the statue of Abraham Lincoln gazes down on the tiny figures of the sightseers.**

Top right and facing page: the Supreme Court of the United States. Designed by Cass Gilbert along classical lines and completed in 1935, this beautifully proportioned white marble building, with its rows of Corinthian columns, is reminiscent of a Greek temple. *Above:* the dramatically illuminated figure of Lincoln, enthroned in Henry Bacon's majestic memorial. *Right:* the memorial to those of the Second Division who lost their lives in the Great War.

The annual blooming of the Japanese cherry blossom marks the unofficial beginning of spring in the capital. Each year thousands of visitors flock to Washington to enjoy the spectacle which owes much to the efforts of Mrs. William Howard Taft, as well as the kindness of the people of Tokyo who, in 1912, presented the city with a gift of 3,000 cherry trees.

The National Air and Space Museum *these pages* houses the world's finest collection of aeronautical as well as astronautical exhibits. Because of its sheer size, only a small part of the collection can be displayed at any one time and many exhibits are frequently loaned to other museums throughout the world. Shown *facing page* is a section of the Air Transportation Gallery where commercial aircraft – from the Pitcairn Mailwing to the important Douglas DC 3 – are imaginatively displayed. The galleries devoted to space exploration *this page* have about them an air of the science-fictional.

Spot-lit against the darkening evening skies, Washington's monuments *these pages* appear even more breathtaking than they do in the full light of day; the massive dome of the Capitol *below* taking on an uncharacteristically light, floating quality.

Home of the nation's First Family and executive office of the President, the famous White House *these pages* was so named in 1814, when the exterior had to be heavily painted to cover the fire damage left by the British.

Topped by the 19½ foot statue of Freedom, the tiered dome of the magnificent Capitol towers over all other Washington buildings. Since the cornerstone was first laid in 1793 the structure has continuously grown and changed. The distinctive and ornate cast iron dome was added in 1865 and extensions to the East Front *facing page and far right* were completed in 1962. More important than the building itself, however, is the work of government that goes on within its chambers.

This page: above spectators watch the guard of honor marching past the Tomb of the Unknowns. This memorial commemorates the unknown fallen warriors from two World Wars and the Korean War. *Top right* a member of the Old Guard, the oldest active infantry unit of the U. S. Army, changes guard every hour. *Top center* the simple grave of Senator Robert Kennedy. *Right* rows of white tombstones cover the hillside in Arlington Cemetery, with the Washington Monument in the background. *Far right and opposite page:* when the U. S. Marines fought their way to the top of Mount Suribachi on Iwo Jima, in 1945, photographer Joe Rosenthal was there to record the historic moment when Old Glory was raised. The statue, by Felix De Waldron, was based on the photograph and is the U. S. Marine Corps War Memorial.

Ringed at its base by 50 star-spangled banners *below,* **one for each State of the Union, the Washington Monument** *far right, bottom right and facing page,* **appears to symbolise the enduring unity of the Nation. The massive obelisk stands halfway between the Capitol and the Lincoln Memorial** *right,* **and is the tallest stone and masonry structure in the world. The peak of the 555 foot column can be reached by either stairs or elevator and the windows in the point's four sides offer unparalleled views of the city and its surroundings.**

Above: **one of approximately 75 modern sculptures to be found in the terraced Sculpture Garden that forms an intrinsic part of the Hirshhorn Museum.** *Facing page:* **the Great Rotunda on the main floor of the National Gallery of Art.**

Overlooking the Tidal Basin *left* and built on land reclaimed from the Potomac River, the Jefferson Memorial *facing page* conforms to the architectural ideals favored by the great statesmen. *Top left:* the Lincoln Memorial and its 36 Doric-style columns, each representing a state in the Union at the time of the Presidents death. *Above:* the Capitol, Washington's crowning glory, seen at its eastern end.

The Capitol Building interior is no less impressive than the much photographed and familiar exterior *facing page.* Shown *above and left* is the magnificent Statuary Hall which served as the chamber of the House of Representatives until 1857. The statues in the Hall, first introduced in 1864, are of notables from each of the nation's states. Dominating this imposing semi-circular chamber designed by Benjamin Latrobe is the beautifully restored dome which was inspired by that of the Pantheon in Rome. *Top left*: the bronze statue of George Washington stands in the enormous Rotunda or Central Hall. It is in the Rotunda that the nation has paid final tribute to 24 of its sons, including Presidents Lincoln and Kennedy.

Originally housed in the vaulted crypts under the Capitol and moved to the Old Senate Chamber in 1860, the Supreme Court of the United States was finally housed in its present building *these pages* in 1935. The carvings on the pediment *above and facing page* depict 'Liberty Enthroned' and at the entrance on the building's west side can be seen the massive bronze doors whose carved panels *above center and facing page* show historic scenes of the development of the law.

The beautiful Jefferson Memorial centers round a gigantic 19 foot-high bronze statue *these pages,* raised on a 6 foot pedestal of black granite, of the third President shown addressing the Continental Congress. The four interior walls of the memorial carry excerpts from Jefferson's writings, including part of the Declaration of Independence.

WE HOLD THESE TRUTHS TO BE SELF-EVIDENT: THAT ALL MEN ARE CREATED EQUAL. THAT THEY ARE ENDOWED BY THEIR CREATOR WITH CERTAIN INALIENABLE RIGHTS. AMONG THESE ARE LIFE, LIBERTY AND THE PURSUIT OF HAPPINESS. THAT TO SECURE THESE RIGHTS GOVERNMENTS ARE INSTITUTED AMONG MEN. WE ··· SOLEMNLY PUBLISH AND DECLARE, THAT THESE COLONIES ARE AND OF RIGHT OUGHT TO BE FREE AND INDEPENDENT STATES ··· AND FOR THE SUPPORT OF THIS DECLARATION, WITH A FIRM RELIANCE ON THE PROTECTION OF DIVINE PROVIDENCE, WE MUTUALLY PLEDGE OUR LIVES, OUR FORTUNES AND OUR SACRED HONOUR.

THE MIND OF MAN

I AM NOT AN ADVOCATE FOR FREQUENT CHANGES IN LAWS AND CONSTITUTIONS. BUT LAWS AND INSTITUTIONS MUST GO HAND IN HAND WITH THE PROGRESS OF THE HUMAN MIND. AS THAT BECOMES MORE DEVELOPED, MORE ENLIGHTENED, AS NEW DISCOVERIES ARE MADE, NEW TRUTHS DISCOVERED AND MANNERS AND OPINIONS CHANGE, WITH THE CHANGE OF CIRCUMSTANCES, INSTITUTIONS MUST ADVANCE ALSO TO KEEP PACE WITH THE TIMES. WE MIGHT AS WELL REQUIRE A MAN TO WEAR STILL THE COAT WHICH FITTED HIM WHEN A BOY AS CIVILIZED SOCIETY TO REMAIN EVER UNDER THE REGIMEN OF THEIR BARBAROUS ANCESTORS.

Contrasted against a clear blue sky, the blossom-laden
bough of a cherry tree overhangs the rippling waters of
the Tidal Basin. *Above:* two of the 50 flags that flutter at
the base of the Washington Monument.

IN THIS TEMPLE
AS IN THE HEARTS OF THE PEOPLE
FOR WHOM HE SAVED THE UNION
THE MEMORY OF ABRAHAM LINCOLN
IS ENSHRINED FOREVER

Like Washington's other memorials to the great statesmen of the nation, the one dedicated to Abraham Lincoln is truly epic in its proportions. Carved from 28 blocks of white marble, the figure itself took sculptor Daniel Chester French four years to complete. At night, bathed in shadow and the yellow glow of the spotlights *facing page*, the figure appears particularly impressive.

Turned golden by the setting sun, the Capitol's west front overlooks the Grant Memorial and its Reflecting Pool *facing page. Top left:* the ultra-modern Children's Hospital. *Top right:* shown left of picture is the famous St. John's Church also known as the Church of the Presidents. *Above left:* the ornate facade of the Library of Congress. *Above right:* the National Visitor Center, formerly Union Station, provides an information service for all visitors to the city. *Overleaf:* the Lincoln Memorial by night.

The famous Marine Corps War Memorial *left, bottom left and facing page* is located outside the northern boundary of Arlington Cemetery. Its splendid statue graphically recalls the heroism and sacrifice of the many who took part in the fierce battle for the Japanese stronghold on Iwo Jima. The flag on the memorial is raised and lowered each day by a Marine Corps color guard. *Far left:* the broad Mall sweeps sedately towards the nation's seat of power. *Below:* a replica of the famous Liberty Bell; traditional symbol of U.S. freedom. The original is housed in Independence Hall, Philadelphia.

Unable to accommodate its constantly growing collection, the classical main building of the National Gallery of Art *far left* has been supplemented by the ultra-modern, I. M. Pei designed, East Building *remaining pictures.* The interior of the new structure *left* makes maximum use of daylight to show off its many fine exhibits and is linked to the original West Building by a cobbled plaza studded with the pyramid shapes of skylights.

Over 1200 churches representing some 70 denominations are to be found in and around Washington. One of the newest and largest of these is the ornate-domed National Shrine of the Immaculate Conception *right*, whose main altar is shown *above*. *Facing page:* the Altar of the Most Holy Trinity in the Byzantine-style monastery Church of Mount St. Sepulchre.

Painted with lights on the sky's limitless canvas, Washington's monuments and buildings take on a strangely etheral quality.

Immaculately restored to its original glory, Ford's Theatre *facing page* is the scene of the assassination of Abraham Lincoln. Shot from behind by the actor John Wilkes Booth, the injured President was taken from his flag-draped box to the Petersen House across the street *below* where he died the following morning. The Watergate Complex *left* is a more recent attraction, its name synonymous with political scandal. *Bottom left:* the Kennedy Center for the Performing Arts casts its colored lights on the Potomac River.

The Monument *right* commemorates Spencer Fullerton Baird, second Secretary of the Smithsonian Institution, who was instrumental in the development of the museums. The Institution's original red-sandstone building *facing page*, because of the unusual Norman style of the architecture, is frequently called the 'Castle in the Mall.' *Far right*: the columns and pediment of the National Archives Building. *Bottom right*: the Robert A. Taft Memorial. The simple tower contains a 27-bell carillon that chimes twice daily. *Below*: the Museum of Natural History.

The statue of General **Andrew Jackson** *below and facing page,* **which stands in Lafayette Park, has the distinction of being the first equestrian statue by an American artist. Jackson is shown in the uniform he wore at the Battle of New Orleans where he defeated the British forces attacking the city. Fine views of the north side of the White House can be had from this point in the park.** *Right and far right:* **the Capitol and the White House: symbols of a city, a nation and democracy.** *Bottom right:* **the Zero Milestone, which stands in the Ellipse, marks the spot from which all distances from Washington to other cities are measured.**

Right: the interior of the Capitol's huge dome, with the beautiful fresco by Brumidi at its center. *Above:* the dome and lantern of the Library of Congress, 125 feet above the floor of the main reading room. *Facing page:* Mount Vernon, George Washington's splendid colonial-style plantation home, stands on the banks of the Potomac in Virginia.

Whether viewed from the east or the west, by day or by night, the incomparable Capitol *these pages* never fails to impress.

Housed in the Rotunda of the National Archives Building *left* are the nation's most sacred documents: the Declaration of Independence, the Constitution and the Bill of Rights. *Below:* the Mormon Tabernacle at Kensington in Maryland. *Bottom:* housed in a granite and marble building in Kentucky is the log cabin where Lincoln, one of the White House's most prestigious occupants, is believed to have been born. *Bottom left and facing page:* the magnificent Jefferson and Lincoln Memorials.

Seat of the United States Government since 1800 and great cultural center of the nation, Washington is a city rich in classical monuments. The city is more than a museum, however, it is a living and growing capital with a respect for the past and its sights keenly set on the future.

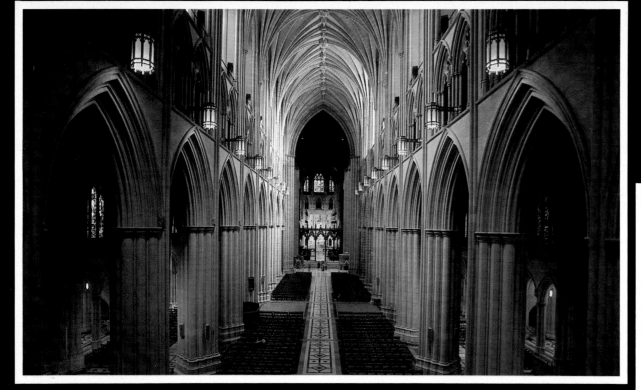

Situated on the highest ground in the city, the massive Washington National Cathedral *these pages* is living proof of the enduring skills of modern craftsmen. The soaring tower, graceful flying buttresses and majestic Gothic arches, whilst based on the concepts of medieval European church architecture are, nevertheless, highly original in their design. The superb *Gloria in Excelsis* Tower *facing page* is fitted with a 53-bell carillon as well as a 10-bell 'ring' and the ring of the Cathedral bells is one of the city's most memorable sounds.

The splendid interiors of Washington's public buildings *these pages* are as varied and imposing as their exteriors.

The two faces of a nation's capital: imposing but impersonal seat of power *above* **and the homely cobbled streets and welcoming houses of historic Georgetown** *facing page.* **The Lincoln Memorial** *overleaf* **appears to glow in the failing light of an autumn landscape.**